How to use Explore

G000071316

In this issue

The 91 daily readings in this issue of *Explore* are designed to help you understand and apply the Bible as you read it each day.

It's serious!

We suggest that you allow 15 minutes each day to work through the Bible passage with the notes. It should be a meal, not a snack! Readings from other parts of the Bible can throw valuable light on the study passage. These cross-references can be skipped if you are already feeling full up, but will expand your grasp of the Bible. *Explore* uses the NIV2011 Bible translation, but you can also use it with the NIV1984 or ESV translations.

Sometimes a prayer box will encourage you to stop and pray through the lessons—but it is always important to allow time to pray for God's Spirit to bring his word to life, and to shape the way we think and live through it.

We're serious!

All of us who work on Explore share a passion for getting the Bible into people's lives. We fiercely hold to the Bible as God's word— to honour and follow, not to explain away.

1 Find ... can read the Bible each day

2 Find a place where you can be quiet and think

3 Ask God to help you understand

4 Carefully read through the Bible passage for today

5 Study the verses with Explore, taking time to think

6 Pray about what you have read

thegoodbook COMPANY

Opening up the Bible

Welcome to Explore

Being a Christian isn't a skill you learn, like carpentry or flower arranging. Nor is it a lifestyle choice, like the kind of clothes you wear, or the people you choose to hang out with. It's about having a real relationship with the living God through his Son, Jesus Christ. The Bible tells us that this relationship is like a marriage.

It's important to start with this, because many Christians view the practice of daily Bible-reading as a Christian duty, or a hard discipline that is just one more thing to get done in our busy modern lives.

But the Bible is God speaking to us: opening his mind to us on how he thinks, what he wants for us and what his plans are for the world. And most importantly, it tells us what he has done for us in sending his Son, Jesus Christ, into the world. It's the way the Spirit shows Jesus to us, and changes us as we behold his glory.

The Bible is not a manual. It's a love letter. And as with any love letter, we'll want to treasure it, and make time to read and re-read it, so we know we are loved, and discover how we can please the One who loves us. Here are a few suggestions for making your daily time with God more of a joy than a burden:

- ❤ *Time:* Find a time when you will not be disturbed, and when the cobwebs are cleared from your mind. Many people have found that the morning is the best time as it sets you up for the day. If you're not a "morning person", then last thing

at night or a mid-morning break might suit you. Whatever works for you is right for you.

- ❤ *Place:* Jesus says that we are not to make a great show of our religion *(see Matthew 6:5-6),* but rather, to pray with the door to our room shut. Some people plan to get to work a few minutes earlier and get their Bible out in an office or some other quiet corner.

- ❤ *Prayer:* Although *Explore* helps with specific prayer ideas from the passage, try to develop your own lists to pray through. Use the flap inside the back cover to help with this. And allow what you read in the Scriptures to shape what you pray for yourself, the world and others.

- ❤ *Share:* As the saying goes: *expression deepens impression.* So try to cultivate the habit of sharing with others what you have learned. Why not join our Facebook group to share your encouragements, questions and prayer requests? Search for *Explore: For your daily walk with God.*

And remember, *it's quality, not quantity, that counts:* better to think briefly about a single verse than to skim through pages without absorbing anything, because it's about developing your relationship with the living God. The sign that your daily time with God is real is when you start to love him more and serve him more wholeheartedly.

Tim Thornborough and Carl Laferton
Editors

1 SAMUEL: Coming king

In the Hebrew Bible, 1 Samuel 1:1 follows Judges 21:25: "In those days Israel had no king; everyone did as they saw fit."

So we are expecting to hear about God providing a king. But instead we are given the story of one woman's private grief.

Read 1 Samuel 1:1-8

❓ *What makes Hannah downhearted?*

Whatever the medical causes for Hannah's barrenness, we are told that ultimately it was God who had closed her womb (v 5-6). God is sovereign over suffering. The question is how to respond to this truth.

❓ *What does Peninnah do (v 6)?*
❓ *What does Elkanah do (v 5, 8)?*
❓ *What do you think they should have done and said?*
❓ *What do you think you would do if you were in Hannah's situation?*

True prayer

Read 1 Samuel 1:9-16

For Hannah, her suffering is a reason to pray. God's sovereignty spurs her into action: if God has closed her womb, then maybe God might also open it.

❓ *How does Hannah feel as she prays?*
❓ *How does she express those feelings?*
❓ *How does she show her faith in God?*

Apply

Some claim that true prayer is about quietness and contemplation. But Hannah's prayer is not like that at all. To pray well we have to have a deep sense of our need.

We also need a deep sense of God's care. Prayer is a cry of faith, arising from the belief that God is our Father, who is able (powerful enough) and willing (loving enough) to answer.

❓ *What stops you from praying? Is it harder to pray when life is difficult or when it's easy?*
❓ *Do you ever think of prayer as a technique you have to learn? How does Hannah's prayer counter that view?*

Read 1 Samuel 1:17-20

Hannah does not yet know how God will answer her prayer. But the point is that she has prayed; and now she is happy to leave it with him.

Hannah's attitude towards God gives us an example to follow. She knows he is sovereign. She wants to do as he sees fit. She illustrates the way the people of Israel should have been relating to God.

Pray

Use Philippians 4:6-7 to help you pray:

"Do not be anxious about anything, but in every situation, by prayer and petition, with thanksgiving, present your requests to God. And the peace of God, which transcends all understanding, will guard your hearts and your minds in Christ Jesus."

Making good his word

Hannah's story is not told to illustrate ordinary life. It is told because it points to something bigger—something literally extra-ordinary.

Read 1 Samuel 1:21-28

❓ *How have Hannah's feelings changed now?*

❓ *What is her attitude towards God?*

In verse 23 Elkanah says, "May the LORD make good his word". This is odd. Hannah is the one who needs to make good her vow. God has not said anything at all!

In fact, the word the Lord has given is his word to his people: the promise to bless them and make them a blessing to the nations. This becomes clearer in the song Hannah sings in chapter 2.

Bigger stories
Read 1 Samuel 2:1-10

❓ *How does Hannah reflect on her own situation in this song?*

❓ *What reversals can you spot—changes from the way things were before?*

❓ *Which verses seem particularly surprising for a new mother to sing?*

Hannah moves beyond her personal experience to the experience of God's people as a whole. Her story is a miniature version of Israel's story—and, indeed, humanity's story.

Hannah is part of that bigger story. Her son, Samuel, will re-establish God's rule over God's people. He will deliver them from their enemies and judge them with justice.

We too need Hannah's story and song as a reminder that the gospel will triumph and God will vindicate his name. In some ways the church in our generation appears to be barren, lacking converts. This should turn us to the Lord in prayer, just like Hannah.

The King

Hannah concludes her song by talking about God's king. She is pointing our attention forward in the story—both within 1 Samuel (to Saul and David) and to God's ultimate King, Jesus.

Read Luke 1:46-55

❓ *How does Mary's song echo Hannah's?*

❓ *How did Jesus fulfil what Hannah sang about?*

⌄ Apply

There are two types of people: those who defy or ignore God and those who humble themselves before him. The message of Hannah's song is that if you are poor or weak or suffering because you have made choices that put God first instead of yourself, it is worth it. The Lord "raises the poor ... and makes them inherit a throne of honour" (1 Samuel 2:8). He exalted Jesus, and this is the first step in turning the world upside down.

❓ *God's King has come. How will you allow that to make a difference to you today?*

Good priest, bad priest

Part of God's solution for sin in Israel was the provision of priests and sacrifices. A priest could make a sacrifice on your behalf to make up for what you had done wrong.

The problem was that, far from pointing the way back to God, the priests were leading the way in turning from him.

Read 1 Samuel 2:11 – 3:1

- ❷ *In 2:13-14, how are the priests exploiting their position?*
- ❷ *In verses 15-16, what do they do that is even worse?*

The fat of the animal was the Lord's portion (see Leviticus 3:3-4, 9-10, 14-16). Eli's sons were stealing from God.

- ❷ *What are the signs of corruption in 1 Samuel 2:22-25?*

Judgment

- ❷ *In verses 27-28, what does the man say God has done for Eli and his family?*
- ❷ *How have Eli and his sons responded?*

Eli has confronted his sons about their sexual immorality, but his leadership is ineffectual. In fact, verse 29 says that he has knowingly benefited from their crimes. We may feel sympathetic for a father who cannot change the heart of his sons; but Eli is also a high priest who could have ended their employment in the tabernacle. But he did not.

God promised in Numbers 25:10-13 that the house of Aaron would be a lasting priesthood. But now this branch of that house would be brought to an end. Priests were supposed to reconcile people with God, but the house of Aaron would never do that effectively.

- ❷ *What is the difference between 1 Samuel 2:11 and 3:1?*

A faithful priest

Interwoven throughout this story are snippets about Samuel, who grows up in the temple.

- ❷ *Find all the verses that mention him. How is he presented?*

So Samuel was qualified to serve in the temple, but not to be a priest. Yet here he is presented in priest-like terms.

Samuel's rise is a sign of the fall of Eli's family. But it also shows that God can raise up a priest from outside the house of Aaron (2:35). Ultimately this is an allusion to Jesus: an eternal priest, "holy, blameless, pure ... [who] sacrificed for sins once for all when he offered himself" (Hebrews 7:26-27).

- ❷ *So what is the answer to Eli's question in 1 Samuel 2:25?*

⌃ Pray

Confess your sins to Jesus, having confidence that he is faithful and just and can purify you from all unrighteousness (1 John 1:9). Know that in him you have forgiveness and freedom.

A coming prophet

Are you ever tempted to wonder, "Why can't God just SPEAK?"

In our lives, our churches and our society, it can seem to us that God is silent or powerless. Chapter 3 opens with a similar picture.

Read 1 Samuel 3:1-10

> ❓ *Where do we see darkness and silence in verses 1-3?*

In verse 4, the silence ends. Samuel hears an audible voice calling him.

> ❓ *The first three times Samuel is called, what does he think? Why (v 7)?*
> ❓ *What is different about the fourth time the Lord calls?*
> ❓ *How does this show a total reversal of the situation in verse 1?*

God's call in verse 10 echoes his call to Moses from the burning bush: "Moses! Moses!" (Exodus 3:4). Moses replied as Samuel does: "Here I am". God is calling Samuel just as he called Moses: to be a prophet, bringing God's word to his people.

A word in crisis

Read 1 Samuel 3:11 – 4:1a

> ❓ *What specific word does God give Samuel (3:11-14)?*
> ❓ *What do we learn about the words God gives Samuel in general (3:19 – 4:1a)?*

Israel was in desperate crisis. There was no ruler, and tabernacle worship was horribly compromised. What did God do? He sent his word. He raised up a prophet.

This is what God always does. In every crisis, it is God's word that we need. It is God's word that refreshes the soul, makes us wise, restores joy to our hearts and gives light to our eyes (Psalm 19:7-8).

···· **TIME OUT** ···

Read Hebrews 1:1-3

> ❓ *In what ways does this show Jesus to be similar to what we have just read about Samuel?*
> ❓ *How is Jesus better than prophets like Samuel?*

Jesus is the word of God. God has spoken through his Son. And we see Jesus in all the Scriptures: the Old Testament is the Spirit-inspired promise of his coming in the Old Testament, and the New Testament is the record of his coming.

⌄ Apply

If it seems that the word of God is rare today, it is not because God is silent. It is because Christians will not speak and people will not listen.

> ❓ *What tempts you to lose confidence in the power and truth of God's word?*
> ❓ *Is that thing actually as powerful and trustworthy as God's word?*
> ❓ *How is God speaking to you through his word today?*

EASTER: Eight words

Last words are often significant. Jesus' last words are eternally so. So this Easter, we're looking at his seven "sayings" from the cross—and one from three days later.

Each "word" gives us a glimpse of the reason for the crucifixion, the character of the man who endured it and the blessings that flow to us from it.

Before we focus in on the scene of the cross, it's helpful to enter into the story so far. If you have time, **read Luke 22:39 – 23:31.**

Forgive them

Read Luke 23:32-34

❓ *Think about this scene from the perspective of...*
  • *the soldiers: what do they think they're doing?*
  • *the Father: what are the soldiers actually doing? Why is this terrible?*
  • *Jesus: what does he think or feel about them? Why is this incredible?*

❓ *Read Isaiah 53:7-8 and 12b, and Psalm 22:18. In what ways are the soldiers unwittingly fulfilling Scripture?*

The efficiency of Luke's description reflects the efficiency of the job itself. It's business as usual for these soldiers as they string up that day's criminals: one, two, three—job done. Yet, as Jesus' clothes are stripped away and his hands impaled and his dignity removed, his chief concern is not his painful humiliation but the souls of the very people inflicting it because, from the view of heaven, these brief verses describe a despicable crime of cosmic proportions.

And yet, remarkably, it was out of love for these soldiers—and for every sinner blind to their rejection of a holy God—that the Father planned to send the Son, and the Son willingly came. **Read Romans 5:8.**

▼ Apply

There are two truths we must hold in tension. First, we are totally responsible for our sin, and second, we are utterly helpless to do anything about it; so we are completely at the mercy of God. Even as Christians, we fail to see the depths of our sin. Think about it: if we had to identify and confess every specific sin we had committed in order to be forgiven of it, what hope would we have?

But we have this hope: a Saviour who paid for us, and who prays for us—"Father, forgive them"—and a Father who delights to show mercy.

❓ *How does this humble you? How does it make you grateful?*

As each study this week will be focused on a single verse, try to memorise each day's "saying". You could write it somewhere you will see it or set a reminder on your phone, so that you can pause and pray about what you've been reflecting on later in the day.

▲ Pray

As you go about your day today, look for opportunities to echo Jesus' prayer for the people around you.

Bible in a year: Leviticus 4-5 • Hebrews 7 ✔

You will be with me

They say that looks can be deceiving. That has never been more true than on Golgotha's hill.

Read Luke 23:35-42

❷ *Look at verses 35, 37, 38, 39. What conclusion have people come to about...*
 • *who Jesus really is (or isn't)?*
 • *what he should do?*
❷ *What conclusion has the second criminal come to (v 40-42)?*
❷ *What does he admit about himself?*

The bystanders look at Jesus—bloodied, beaten and gasping for breath—and conclude that he is exactly what he looks like: a sham Messiah; no king at all.

The second criminal looks at Jesus—bloodied, beaten and gasping for breath—and by faith sees the King who will one day ascend his throne and rule with power. So, as the bystanders jeer at Jesus, "Save yourself!" this man turns and pleads with Jesus, *Save me*. And he is rewarded with the most wonderful promise...

Read Luke 23:43

These are familiar words—but it's worth pausing to chew them over.

❷ *Reflect on the significance of each of these phrases in turn. Why were they good news in the ear of this criminal?*
 • *"Truly I tell you"*   • *"today"*
 • *"you will be with me"* • *"in paradise"*

⌄ Apply

Jesus refused to save himself so that he could save *you*. If we too admit our guilt, recognise Jesus' authority and cry out to him for rescue, we receive the same promise: "Truly I tell you [on the day of your death] you will be with me in paradise".

❷ *What about this encounter gives us particular hope when we're feeling...*
 • *discouraged by our sin and by the way we keep letting God down?*
 • *the weakness of our bodies or the nearness of death?*

In some ways we can have even greater confidence than that criminal. Jesus no longer looks at us from the cross but from his throne in heaven (Revelation 1). He is risen, ascended and coming back as King—and he will take you to be with him for ever.

⌃ Pray

There is a fountain filled with blood
Drawn from Immanuel's veins;
And sinners, plunged beneath that flood,
Lose all their guilty stains.

The dying thief rejoiced to see
That fountain in his day;
And there may I, though vile as he,
Wash all my sins away.

When this poor lisping, stammering tongue
Lies silent in the grave,
Then in a nobler, sweeter song,
I'll sing thy power to save.

("There is a fountain", William Cowper)

Woman, behold your son

A crucifixion was a bloody, distressing spectacle. Here the apostle John tells us about some women with strong stomachs and devoted hearts...

Full family

Read John 19:25-27

❓ *Who, does John tell us, was watching Jesus die (v 25)? Why, do you think?*

❓ *What does Jesus say to Mary (his mother) and John ("the disciple whom he loved")? Why, do you think?*

❓ *Why does John choose to include this in his Gospel, do you think? What point might he be making? (See John 20:30-31 for John's "editorial process".)*

In his moment of greatest agony, Jesus shows concern for his mother. He sees a woman who is about to lose her son, and ensures that she has someone to care for her. He sees a disciple who is about to lose his best friend, and ensures that he has someone to love and be loved by.

✔ Apply

There is something wonderfully human about this. Jesus experienced the full depth of relationships that we do. He knows what it's like to watch someone you love face loss—that gut-level instinct to do whatever you can to help. And yet, as always, Jesus shows us humanity in full perfection. When we are in physical pain or under emotional stress, we often retreat in self-pity or lash out in resentment. But Jesus continued to look out in compassion.

❓ *In what sense is this a comfort to you? In what sense is it a challenge?*

New family

There is also a bigger point to be made here. After all, we know that Jesus had other brothers and sisters who could have taken care of Mary (Matthew 13:55-56). And if this was primarily about a long-term care package, it could have been put in place before this moment or after Jesus' resurrection. Besides, Jesus' words are not so much a request (*Please look after Mary when I'm gone*) as a statement of fact ("Here is your mother"). So this saying from the cross is also a hint at what Jesus' death will achieve: it will bind his followers together as family.

New families are formed at the foot of the cross (Ephesians 2:14-22). Our Lord's blood creates ties that are thicker than water.

✔ Apply

Read 1 John 3:16-18

❓ *Is there someone in your church family whom Jesus would have you take "into [your] home"?*

❓ *What would it look like to genuinely treat them as your new son/mother/brother/sister?*

Start by praying for them now. And then call them or message them!

My God, my God…

Pause a moment to consider this: what would it feel like to be abandoned by the person you most love in your hour of greatest need—and to know their displeasure?

That gives us a small sense of the emotional force behind today's word from the cross.

Read Matthew 27:32-50

> ❷ Look at v 46. What is significant about…
> • what Jesus says?
> • the way Jesus says it?
> ❷ What is the evidence that Jesus has indeed been forsaken by God (v 43, 45— see Amos 8:9 for the significance of darkness)?

These words are not a whimper but a deep cry of anguish. This is the only time in the synoptic Gospels when Jesus does not address God as his Father. The bystanders mishear Jesus' cry to "Eli" and think he's calling "Elijah" (who Jewish tradition said would appear from heaven to help in times of trouble).

There are scarcely any words that can describe Jesus' agony. So it's significant that he reaches for Israel's songbook, the Psalms, to put words to the experience.

Read Psalm 22:1-21

> ❷ What similarities do you see between Psalm 22 and the scene in Matthew? Find as many as you can.

For every hour of his life so far, Jesus has experienced only the love, delight and pleasure of his Father. But for these three dark and lonely hours, Jesus now experiences the full weight of God's anger at sin.

> ❷ What, then, is the answer to Jesus'

question in Matthew 27:46—"My God, why…"?

Why? Jesus knows the answer to his own question, of course. He is willingly drinking the cup of God's wrath (Matthew 26:39); he is giving "his life as a ransom for many" (20:28). In that moment, "God made him who had no sin to be sin for us, so that in him we might become the righteousness of God" (2 Corinthians 5:21).

⌄ Apply

Why did God forsake Christ? So that he can welcome you. So that you can enjoy the love, delight and pleasure of the Father every day of your life. Even in those times when you are too distressed to sleep (Psalm 22:2)… even when you are scorned by others (v 6)… even when your body is broken and your heart is faint (v 14)… Even then, you are not forsaken, because Christ became the forsaken man of Psalm 22 for you.

> ❷ When God feels far away or as if he doesn't love you…
> • what hope does Matthew 27 give you to remember?
> • what words does Psalm 22 give you to pray?

⌃ Pray

Read through Psalm 22:1-21 again, thanking Jesus for enduring each specific agony for your sake.

I am thirsty

Try to remember a time when you were really, really thirsty. How would describe the sensation, and the thoughts or feelings that accompanied it?

Before we turn back to John's crucifixion account, let's trace the theme of "thirst" through his Gospel so far.

The well

Read John 4:4-14

❷ *Who is thirsty (v 7)?*
❷ *What kind of water does Jesus tell the woman she can have, if she asks (v 10)?*
❷ *Where do we get that kind of water, and what does it give us (v 13-14)?*

So Jesus is moving the conversation from physical thirst to spiritual thirst.

❷ *What exactly does it mean to be spiritually thirsty, do you think? How is that like physical thirst?*

The river

Read John 7:37-39

❷ *Who is "thirsty" here?*
❷ *What's the solution to this spiritual thirst (v 38)? Where do we get it, and what does it do for us?*
❷ *What had to happen before people could receive this "living water" (end v 39)?*

Run dry

Read John 19:28-29

The Scripture that John has in mind here, as Jesus hangs on the cross, is probably Psalm 22:15.

❷ *Who is "thirsty" now?*
❷ *What do these words tell us about what the cross is achieving?*

Every human knows what it is to be thirsty; and every human knows what it is to be spiritually thirsty. Ever since Eden, we've rejected the Lord—the fount of "living water", who alone can keep us spiritually alive—and dug our own broken cisterns (Jeremiah 2:13). Like the woman at the well, we look to other people to satisfy us with their love or approval or admiration. But it doesn't work. Our thirst is killing us.

Not so for Jesus: he was a man whose soul sprang with life and vitality, in dependence on his Father and in the power of the Spirit. Yet on the cross he not only endured physical thirst but took on himself our spiritual condition: "I am thirsty". And in so doing, he opened up a spring of living water for anyone who would come to him and drink.

His thirst brought water; his death brought life. This was the moment of his greatest glory (John 7:39; 12:23). Will you come to him and drink?

⌄ Apply

❷ *Jesus thirsted so that you could drink. How should that change the way you think and feel about the other places you go to for satisfaction?*
❷ *What will it look like for you to come to him and drink?*

It is finished

Hitting "send" on a big work project... emptying the ironing basket... completing an application process... Few words are as satisfying as this one: "FINISHED!"

Read John 19:30

> ❷ *"It is finished." How might those words have sounded to those watching the crucifixion?*
> ❷ *How should they sound to believers on Good Friday 2020, do you think?*

The Greek word is *tetelestai*—finished, completed, done. In New Testament times it was written on business receipts to indicate that they were paid in full. This is no note of surrender but rather a cry of triumph—Christ's saving work is finished. The sin of his people is paid for, in full, for ever.

···· TIME OUT

As with so much in this scene, we can hear in these words from the cross an echo of psalm 22. We read the first part of this Psalm two days ago—a song of immense suffering, rejection and despair. But then there's a shift as the tone changes, and the psalm becomes a song of triumph.

Read Psalm 22:22-31

> ❷ *What does this psalm hint that Jesus will achieve on the cross (v 26, 27, 29)?*

▼ Apply

Sometimes we are haunted by past mistakes that seem too much for mercy. But Jesus says, "It is finished". There is no debt too big for him to pay.

Sometimes we mess up "big time"—or for the umpteenth time—and imagine that we need to withdraw from the Lord for a while until our guilt has "worn off". But Jesus says, "It is finished". You can run to him in repentance immediately and enjoy his forgiveness instantly.

Sometimes we get mired in feelings of resentment or jealousy that we can't seem to move on from. But Jesus says, "It is finished". He's set you free from sin, so you don't have to bring it into your day today.

Sometimes we live as if we've got something to prove—if not to God then at least to his people. But Jesus says, "It is finished". You can stop striving because there's nothing left to earn and no other approval that matters.

Sometimes we struggle to forgive other Christians. We keep chewing over the slight or injustice committed against us. But Jesus says, "It is finished". Their penalty is paid in full, so you can entrust this to him.

> ❷ *Which of those scenarios is resonating with you at the moment? Bring it before the Lord in prayer now.*
> ❷ *When else this week might you need to remind yourself, "It is finished"? Make sure you do!*

Father, into your hands

Now we come to Jesus' final breath, and to his final words from the cross.

Luke 23:44-56

"[Jesus] breathed his last" (v 46). Look at the responses Luke portrays for us in the verses that follow:

❷ *What do each of these people think has happened, and what do they expect to happen next, do you think?*
- *The centurion (v 47)*
- *The crowd (v 48)*
- *The women (v 49, 55-56)*
- *Joseph (v 50-54)*

The tearing of the curtain in the temple hints at a victory, but on the hill outside Jerusalem it must look like defeat. Jesus' enemies have finally crushed him. The crowd express their grief but soon move on now that the show's over. Jesus' friends are quietly determined to honour him with a decent burial now that he's gone. The women go home and expect to return with their spices and perfumes after the Sabbath. No revival is anticipated. It's game over. Dead and buried.

But what about Jesus? What did he think would happen next? His final words give us a hint at what he expected to happen after his last breath. Once again, they're taken from a psalm.

Read Psalm 31:1-5

❷ *What is the psalmist's expectation in the face of his enemy's trap?*

Jesus' final words were a prayer to his Father

as, with relief and assurance, he entrusted his soul into his hands. He was confident of deliverance beyond the grave. He had been obedient to his Father throughout life and even unto death (Philippians 2:6-8); so now he was assured of a glorious resurrection and welcome into heaven (Philippians 2:9-11). It wasn't game over but job done.

☑ Apply

❷ *Do you ever contemplate your own moment of death? How does that make you feel?*

Psalm 31:5 isn't just words for King Jesus, but words for his people too. The first Christian martyr, Stephen, prayed something similar as he died (Acts 7:59). There is no safer place for our souls than in our Father's hands.

Because Jesus faced death with obedience, we can face death with confidence. One day, as we die, we too can pray, "Father, into your hands I commit my spirit", assured of deliverance beyond our final breath. There may be pain, but there need be no fear. It will not be game over but job done (Matthew 25:23).

❷ *If we can face death with confidence, how will that shape...*
- *how we face life in the meantime (see Psalm 31:24)?*
- *how we pray for Christians who are currently approaching the end of their life?*

Peace be with you

A very happy Easter! On this Resurrection Sunday, we're looking at two words from that first Resurrection Sunday: one about the risen Jesus and one from the risen Jesus.

The angels' words

Read Luke 24:1-12

❓ *The shocks for these women keep coming, and keep getting bigger. What are they?*
• v 2   • v 3   • v 4   • v 6

❓ *What words of Jesus do the angels remind the women of (v 7)? Why are these significant?*

The women remember Jesus' words and—we can presume—believe them: Jesus has risen, just like he said! But the disciples' do not believe the women's words, because they seem "like nonsense" (v 11).

⌄ Apply

"He has risen." Pause for a moment to think about the implications of those words. How many can you think of? (Can you get to 10? 20?) Here are a couple to get you started:

Jesus has risen, so...

... everything he said was true.

... he is still alive today.

Once you've thought of some more, spend some time in prayer, praising Jesus for each one.

The Saviour's words

Read Luke 24:13-35

Later that day two disciples meet Jesus on the road to Emmaus (v 13-32). When they realise what has happened, they rush back to Jerusalem to tell the others, only to be greeted with the news that Jesus has also appeared to Simon (v 34). There's an excited swapping of stories as the room buzzes with discussion. Then into the hubbub breaks a familiar voice...

Read Luke 24:36-49

❓ *What's surprising about verse 37?! How does Jesus reassure them (v 38-43)?*

❓ *Jesus reminds them of his words (v 44), and then the words of Scripture (v 45-47). Why, do you think?*

We've seen how Jesus was concerned to fulfil Old Testament Scripture as he died. Now that he is risen, he opens the disciples' minds so that they can understand those Scriptures too (v 45). His death was not a sign of his failure but of his status as God's Messiah (a fact confirmed by his resurrection)—and the very means by which he brings forgiveness of sins. This is a message worth sharing (v 48)!

⌄ Apply

"Peace be with you!" Pray again, praising Jesus for the peace with God that you now enjoy, and the presence of God with you by his Spirit that you now experience. Then **read Luke 24:50-53** and head into your day "with great joy"—Jesus is risen, and he's brought you peace!

1 SAMUEL: Weighty

We are back in the book of 1 Samuel, and today's passage poses a simple yet deeply challenging question: how seriously do you take God?

What glory is

In Hebrew the word "glory" comes from the same root as the word "weighty". God's glory is his weightiness—that is, the seriousness with which he must be taken.

Read 1 Samuel 4:1-11

> ❓ *What happens when the Israelites go out to battle for the first time (v 1-2)?*
> ❓ *What do they decide to do the next time (v 3-4)?*

The ark was an ornamented box containing the stone tablets on which Moses recorded the covenant God had made with his people at Sinai, along with a sample of manna. It was a reminder of Israel's covenant obligations, and of God's provision in the past. Above all it was a symbol of God's presence.

The ark had been in the tent of meeting at Shiloh since the conquest of the promised land (Joshua 18:1), but now the Israelites decide to move it. They are taking God lightly, thinking they can co-opt him for their own purposes.

> ❓ *Who does take God seriously here?*
> ❓ *What is the result?*

Stealing glory

Read 1 Samuel 4:12-22

> ❓ *What is the chain of events that follows?*
> ❓ *What does the name Ichabod reveal to be the most significant thing that has happened (v 21)?*

In a sense, God's glory has been stolen by Eli's family, who dishonoured God. The writer draws our attention to Eli's weight (v 18). Remember that Eli and his sons took the fat from the offerings, which belonged to God (2:16, 29). This fattening—stealing the weighty glory of God—leads directly to Eli's death.

A heavy hand

Read 1 Samuel 5:1-6

> ❓ *What is the effect of God's weighty glory in Ashdod?*

Before God all other gods must fall. Only God has substance and weight. All other gods have to be propped up. That includes anything that rivals God in our lives.

🔼 Pray

We worship the same God that we read about in these verses. Worship him now.

Romans 12:1 tells us, "Offer your bodies as a living sacrifice". We owe God not the fat from animal offerings but our whole lives. Ask God to help you see how to worship him in all you do.

🔽 Apply

> ❓ *How seriously do you take God?*
> ❓ *What difference will a right view of his glory make in how you live today?*

From bad to worse

"Who can stand in the presence of the Lᴏʀᴅ?" is the key question in today's passage—and it's as relevant now as it was then.

Read 1 Samuel 5:6 – 6:9

❓ *What does God do to the Philistines (5:6, 9, 12)?*
❓ *What can alleviate their suffering?*

The Philistines cannot live with the glory of God. They are guilty, and it is crushing them. So they decide to send the ark away, pulled by cows whose instincts ought to send them home to their calves in Philistia, yet who head straight for Israel.

This holy God

Read 1 Samuel 6:10 – 7:2

❓ *What do you think the Philistine rulers said to each other when they went home in 6:16?*
❓ *What do you think they expected to happen in Beth Shemesh?*
❓ *Are you surprised by what does happen?*

The ark is safely home in Israel. But the local townspeople disrespectfully look inside it, and the Lord's weight now presses down destructively on his own people.

The people of Beth Shemesh deal with the ark in the same way the Philistines did: they send it away.

Victory

Who can stand in the presence of the holy God? Only those who take his glory seriously. But "all have sinned and fall short of the glory of God" (Romans 3:23). We cannot stand in the presence of the Lord. We will be crushed by him?

True repentance

Read 1 Samuel 7:3-14

❓ *How do the people show that their repentance is genuine (v 3-8)?*
❓ *How does God show that their repentance is effective (v 9-14)?*

To gain victory, we too must put our faith in sacrifice, like the Israelites in verses 8-10. But for us the sacrifice is that of Jesus.

The capture of the ark seemed to be a disaster, but in the morning Dagon lay fallen. Defeat proved to be the means of victory for God. It was the same at the cross. Jesus died, but by his death Satan was defeated. Jesus walked victorious from the tomb.

And if God has helped us "thus far" (v 12), by giving us his own Son, then surely he will bring us safely home to glory.

🔼 Pray

Consider how the story of the Israelites in these chapters—taking God lightly, losing his presence, deserving death, repenting, and finding victory—has been reflected in your own life, and spend time praising God.

Pray also for those you know who have not yet put their trust in Jesus' sacrifice.

A king like the nations

Do you ever wish you were more like everyone else? That is what Israel's elders ask to be in 1 Samuel 8.

Read 1 Samuel 7:13 – 8:5

❷ *How would you describe Israel when ruled by Samuel (7:13-17)?*
❷ *But what is the disappointment at the start of chapter 8?*

The people don't like what is happening. Coming to Samuel, they explain their concerns and ask for a king.

❷ *Is a king a logical answer to the problem of Samuel and his sons?*
❷ *Do you think Samuel's sons are the main reason for requesting a king?*

A king has been anticipated in earlier texts (starting in Genesis 17:6), and so we might expect God to initiate the introduction of a king. But instead it comes as a request from the elders. And they are asking not for God's promised King but for a king "such as all the other nations have".

Rejection

Read 1 Samuel 8:6-22

❷ *Why do you think Samuel is displeased in verse 6?*
❷ *What, does God say, is the elders' motive (v 7-8)?*

Israel had a special identity as God's people, set apart to be a light to the other nations. The elders are rejecting this identity. They are rejecting God as their King.

❷ *How does Samuel describe the future king (v 11-18)?*

❷ *How does that compare to God's rule?*

···· TIME OUT ··

Read Mark 10:45

❷ *How does Jesus compare with the king that Samuel describes?*

---

❷ *What do the people want their king to do for them (1 Samuel 8:20)?*
❷ *How could Samuel have used what has happened in the previous chapters to show them their mistake?*

✅ Apply

The church has inherited Israel's status as God's special people: "You are … a holy nation, God's special possession, that you may declare the praises of him who called you out of darkness into his wonderful light" (1 Peter 2:9). But we, too, have a tendency to look to what we can see rather than trusting in God. Maybe it is other people—their help, their approval—or maybe it is a career or possessions. But these things are tyrants by comparison with God.

❷ *In what areas do you particularly long to be like the individuals or the culture around you?*
❷ *How do those things compare with God?*
❷ *How can knowing the distinct identity that God has given you help you to live contentedly under his rule?*

Secret anointing

Israel has asked for a king "such as all the other nations have". God has said they will have a king. But who will it be? Chapter 9 introduces us to a man named Saul…

Read 1 Samuel 9:1-10

❷ *What opinion of Saul do you think the writer wants us to have here?*

❷ *Does he seem like the king Samuel described in the previous chapter?*

The feast

Read 1 Samuel 9:11-27

❷ *What is the feast for (v 12-13)?*

❷ *How does Samuel treat Saul at the feast (v 17-22)?*

According to Leviticus, the participants in a peace offering like this one ate the meat after it was offered to God. The leg of the offering belonged to the priest (Leviticus 7:33-34). So giving Saul this particular cut of meat shows that he is going to be like a priest—the Lord's anointed one.

There is another big hint about Saul's new status. In this chapter we see Saul repeatedly going up. He goes up to the town (1 Samuel 9:11), up to the high place (v 19), up to the head of the table (v 22), and up to the roof of Samuel's house (v 25). This is significant. The king of Israel is, metaphorically, ascending to his throne.

Anointed

❷ *How would you describe Saul's manner during this chapter?*

❷ *What do you think he is thinking?*

❷ *Samuel seems totally confident about what is happening. Why?*

Read 1 Samuel 10:1

The culmination of this part of the story comes in this verse, as Saul is anointed by Samuel. But this anointing is secret—Samuel sends even Saul's servant away (9:27). The private, domestic scenes in chapter 9 likewise seem a far cry from what was imagined in chapter 8—a powerful king with thousands of soldiers and servants.

This is not so different from what we see in the life of Jesus. At his baptism Jesus is anointed as King (Luke 3:21-22; see Psalm 2:7). But he is not yet acknowledged as King. Instead he is despised and rejected. His exaltation as King must wait.

⌃ Pray

Now Jesus is the ultimate King, ruling with power as the head of the church (Ephesians 1:22). So he will accomplish his purposes for us and for our mission—just as God promised to make Saul a king.

Do you feel the contrast between the glory of Christ the King and the apparent weakness of the church? Do not give up. Christ rules all things.

Pray for your churches, communities, families and friends, knowing that you are on the winning side.

Finding a king

As Saul gradually becomes recognised as king, the question everyone is wondering is: What kind of king he will be?

Read 1 Samuel 10:1-16

❷ *What three signs does Samuel promise (v 1-6)?*
❷ *What does he promise will happen to Saul (v 6-7)? How does this come true?*

The promise is that "God is with" Saul (v 7). He must reign according to God's words—listening to Samuel's instructions (v 8) and hearing from God himself (v 10).

Long live the king

Read 1 Samuel 10:17-27

The secret choice is now made public. God's providence is seen as the lot falls to Saul. The people get the king they asked for.

❷ *What happens next (v 22-23)?*
❷ *How does this episode reflect on Saul?*
❷ *How does it reflect on God?*
❷ *What does it make us think about the people as a whole?*

The people have rejected God's rule yet ask him for help. They need him to find their king!

Samuel explains the rights and duties of the king—we can assume they're different from what he described in 8:11-18. Perhaps, now that he's been found, Saul will after all prove to be the king God's people need.

❷ *How does 10:26-27 present the new king? What is positive? What is negative?*

Judge and king

Read 1 Samuel 11:1-15

❷ *How does Saul's response to the crisis (v 5-7) differ from everyone else's (v 3-4)?*
❷ *What effect does this have on the people (v 7b-12)?*

After the victory, the people "renew the kingship" (v 14). Saul is now truly the king.

❷ *What is his attitude towards the Lord (v 13-15)?*

For now, Saul acts as an old-style judge, mediating the rule of God. There are allusions to previous judges: for example, Bezek, where Saul gathers his army, was the site of the first military victory in Judges (Judges 1:4-5), while Gilgal, where they go after the victory, was the place where Joshua gathered the people to renew the covenant (Joshua 5).

But 1 Samuel 11:15 is a turning point. Instead of being a judge who rescues the people, Saul becomes the king like the nations. From now on, instead of mediating God's rule, he will replace it.

☑ Apply

Because of Jesus, we too now have the Spirit of God in and among us.

❷ *How can you seek to live under God's word and lead other people towards God, as Saul does in chapter 11?*

Bible in a year: Leviticus 26-27 • Revelation 4 ✔

Samuel speaks

The story of Saul's appointment as king ends as it began: with a warning speech from Samuel.

Read 1 Samuel 12:1-5

❓ *Where do you see legal language in this passage?*

❓ *If Samuel is on trial, what is the verdict?*

It soon becomes clear whom the real trial concerns: God versus the people.

By asking for a king to replace God, the people have, in effect, accused God of failing in his divine kingship. The people will be vindicated if God is condemned. But if God is vindicated, then the people will be condemned.

Read 1 Samuel 12:6-18

❓ *What evidence does Samuel present of God's faithfulness (v 6-11)?*

❓ *What evidence is there of the people's unfaithfulness (v 12)?*

With the verdict clear, the judgment is made. Samuel calls upon God, who sends thunder and rain to ruin the wheat harvest.

Do not be afraid

Read 1 Samuel 12:19-25

God is gracious, and the possibility of repentance is still open. When the people repent and ask Samuel to intercede for them, he tells them not to be afraid.

The logic of verse 20 is intriguing. It isn't *You have done evil, so turn back to God*; rather Samuel is saying, *You have turned from God to evil, but do not turn from God to evil.*

Even though they have done evil, he treats them as those who have not yet turned away from God. He seems to be telling them not to think of themselves as hopeless sinners. The judgment does not need to confirm them as people who are "away from the LORD"; they can start again.

❓ *In verses 21-22, how does Samuel highlight the greatness of the Lord?*

❓ *What does Samuel say he will do (v 23)?*

❓ *What does he say the people should do (v 24)?*

❓ *What motivations does he provide for them (v 24-25)?*

This is what it means to be God's people: to "serve him faithfully"—that is, full of faith. As Paul makes clear in Romans 4 and Galatians 3, it is not ethnic identity that defines God's people, but faith in the "great things he has done for [us]". It is not our actions that define us, but God's actions.

▼ Apply

❓ *What are you hoping may "do you ... good" or "rescue" you (1 Samuel 12:21)?*

❓ *What will it look like for you to "not turn away from the LORD, but serve the LORD with all your heart" (v 20)?*

Blessed one

In the next three issues of Explore, we're going to tour the five books of Psalms (the Psalter), enjoying psalms of every type. We start (predictably!) with Psalm 1.

❷ *How do you feel about studying Psalms?*
❷ *What are your expectations?*

Walk, stand, sit

Psalms 1 and 2 are like two grand pillars, one on each side of the entrance gate into the books of Psalms. They introduce Book I and also head up the whole Psalter.

Read Psalm 1:1-6

❷ *What does the blessed one in verses 1-2 do, and not do?*
❷ *What picture of blessedness are we given in verse 3?*

To say "Blessed is the one who..." is confidently to affirm that this person is under the favour of God. And yet, to be "the one who does not" walk, stand or sit with those in verse 1 results in mockery. This person may be blessed, but it comes at a cost.

In verse 3, we are given a beautiful picture of blessedness. In a hot climate, the only vegetation that always bears fruit is a tree with roots deep in life-giving water. Here is someone whose roots go deeply into God, the source of life. You can see the fruit of their roots.

Blessings with warnings

❷ *Why will those who "stand" in verse 1 "not stand" in verse 5?*

❷ *What is the deep reason why the blessings and warnings in this psalm are true (v 6)?*
❷ *How is Jesus the ultimate Psalm-1 man?*

Verses 4-5 warn that there is no other path of blessing. There is a judgment coming. Those who "stand" in verse 1 may seem substantial, even weighty and significant; but on that day they will be seen to be insubstantial, blown away like "chaff" at harvest time. "The LORD", the covenant God, is the reason why both the blessing and the warning are true. He "watches over the way of the righteous".

Only one man truly fits the description of Psalm 1 and deserves to inherit this blessing. When Jesus of Nazareth sang, **"Blessed is the one who..."** he believed it, he lived it and he sought blessing in no other place. He was mocked most sharply, and yet he delighted in his Father's instruction. The covenant God, his Father, watched over his way. So Jesus is the man upon whom the blessing of God the Father rests—the one with whom God the Father was and is well pleased (Matthew 3:17; 17:5).

⌃ Pray

Thank God for inspiring this wonderful book. Ask him to help you to see Jesus more clearly as you sing these psalms. Pray that you would follow him in finding blessing through trust in and obedience to God.

Father and son

Saul's army gains victory again. But this time there is someone else leading them.

Fear
Read 1 Samuel 13:1-15

❓ *How do the soldiers feel (v 6-8)? Why?*

❓ *How would you describe Saul's leadership here?*

You can imagine Saul scanning the horizon for Samuel and watching in horror as more troops desert. In the end, even though only a priest can offer a sacrifice, Saul offers it himself (v 9). He acts as though God will not act. He does not really trust him.

❓ *Who does Saul blame for this (v 11)?*

❓ *What is Samuel's opinion (v 13)?*

A king is needed who obeys God in all circumstances, even under pressure. Saul isn't that man. So his kingdom will not endure.

Faith
Read 1 Samuel 14:1-15 (If you have time, read 13:16 – 14:23)

❓ *What emphasises the Israelites' powerlessness in 13:19-22?*

❓ *So why is Jonathan confident (14:1, 6)?*

Jonathan describes the Philistines as "uncircumcised men" (14:6); so he sees this as a battle between the covenant people of God and the enemies of God. He acts from faith.

❓ *How else does Jonathan show faith in verses 6-12?*

❓ *Why do the Philistines panic in verse 15?*

⌄ Apply

❓ *What brave things are you being called to do for God?*

The son must die
Read 1 Samuel 14:24-46

❓ *Jonathan saw this as a battle for the Lord's honour, but how does Saul describe it (v 24)?*

❓ *What's the result of this attitude (v 24, 31-33)?*

❓ *Do you think Saul is right to blame Jonathan for God's silence (v 37-44)?*

Jonathan is blamed for others' sin. God's silence is the result of Saul's own self-centredness, and of the people's sinful request for a king (see 8:18). A father plans to shed the blood of his own son for the sake of the people; this is a warped version of the story of Jesus. The difference is that Saul really just wants to cover up his own guilt.

In fact Jonathan has already risked his life to save the people. While the army despaired, he crawled into a hole (14:11) and ascended to lead them to victory (v 13-15). He points to the story of the One who leads us through death to life.

⌃ Pray

Reflecting on the similarities and differences between Jonathan and Jesus, praise God for the cross.

The final straw

The whistle-stop tour of Saul's successes at the end of chapter 14 betrays what the writer really wants us to see and spend time on: Saul's continued disobedience.

Judgment

Read 1 Samuel 14:47 – 15:9

Destruction comes to the Amalekites—not because they are Amalekites but because they are sinners.

This should alarm us because we are also sinners. This is a picture of what all humanity deserves, and faces, from God. We don't like to talk about divine judgment because we prefer to minimise human sin. But this is a mistake. It was Saul's mistake, too.

Excuses

Read 1 Samuel 15:10-35

In verse 24a it looks as though Saul is truly repentant. But his repentance is not for real.

- ❓ *What excuses does Saul make in verses 15, 21 and 24?*
- ❓ *How seriously does he expect God to take his disobedience?*
- ❓ *What does verse 30 show to be his main concern?*
- ❓ *What is Samuel's response to all this (v 35)?*

Saul has taken it upon himself to decide what is right and wrong. This is prideful blasphemy. God was the one who appointed Saul as king (v 17), but in verse 12 Samuel discovers that Saul has built a monument to himself. Everything that Saul is, he is because of God's goodness, but he thinks he himself deserves the honour.

Regret

Samuel describes God as consistent (v 29): he doesn't change his mind. Yet God regrets making Saul king (v 11, 35). How can both be true? The key is that *Saul* has changed; he "has turned away" (v 11). God's character does not change, but his response does.

God doesn't change his mind. That means he takes every sin seriously. But he also takes seriously every instance of true repentance. This is what he has promised.

▾ Apply

You may have objections and doubts about what God is like, how seriously to take the Bible (especially difficult passages like the destruction of the Amalekites), and how to obey God. It is good to have questions, but sometimes these can turn into excuses.

- ❓ *Who could you ask to help you to think through these questions and to commit to obeying God?*
- ❓ *What other kinds of excuses do you make for disobedience?*

In prayer, confess your sins and ask for God's help in truly turning back to him.

Enter the shepherd-king

God has already planned his next choice of king. He sends Samuel off to find him. But who will it be?

Read 1 Samuel 16:1-13

> ❓ *How do you think Samuel felt as he travelled to Bethlehem?*
> ❓ *What about on the way home?*

An impressive appearance seems to Samuel like a good qualification. But God brings low those who are high and raises up those who are low (2:7-8). He is looking for humility or lowliness of heart. This is what he finds in David, a shepherd.

···· TIME OUT ····

Throughout the rest of the Bible, this picture of shepherd-leadership is key. In Ezekiel 34:1-24 God promises a new shepherd-king to look after his people. Ultimately this points to Jesus, the good Shepherd, who gave his life for his sheep (John 10:11).

The Spirit
Read 1 Samuel 16:13-23

> ❓ *What happens to David when he is anointed with oil (v 13)?*
> ❓ *In the following verse, what has happened to Saul?*

Saul remains king, but he no longer has God's Spirit, so his authority and abilities begin to fade. David, meanwhile, has an anointing that is different from any previous ruler. The Spirit came upon Saul for specific tasks (10:6, 10; 11:6), but in David's case he is continually and permanently with him.

God sends an evil spirit to torment Saul (16:14). This is probably not a demonic spirit but a spirit that brings misery (another meaning of the word "evil" in Hebrew).

> ❓ *What solution is suggested to this misery?*
> ❓ *How does the description of David change between verses 12 and 18?*

☑ Apply

In Isaiah 11:1-5, a new king from the line of Jesse is promised: one on whom the Spirit of the Lord will rest. Jesus is the fulfilment of this promise. He was anointed as God's Spirit-filled King.

1 John 2:20 and 27 tell us that Christians share this identity: we have an "anointing" and therefore know the truth. Filled with the Spirit, we are called to speak and act on Jesus' behalf.

> ❓ *How might that change your view of what you do and say today?*
> ❓ *How could being like David help us to represent Christ well?*

⌃ Pray
Read Matthew 11:28-29

This is what it means to be under Jesus' kingship. Bring your burdens and needs to him in prayer, asking for his help.

Facing giants

Do you ever feel that the world's problems are just too big? In 1 Samuel 17, the people of God face a problem which is literally gigantic.

Read 1 Samuel 17:19-32 (If you have time, read 17:1-32)

❓ *What impression do we get of the Israelites and of Saul?*

❓ *What does David do, and how is he different from the other Israelites?*

❓ *What view does he have of what is going on?*

Picture the tall yet virtually defeated king with this young shepherd boy standing before him. *Don't lose heart*, says the smaller of the men encouragingly. *I'll fight the giant.*

Read 1 Samuel 17:33-58

❓ *Can you spot the contrasts between armour and weapons, and the power of the Lord?*

❓ *Why does David want to kill Goliath (v 36, 45)?*

❓ *How does the battle turn out after Goliath is dead (v 51-53)?*

Us in the story

Imagine yourself as one of the Israelite soldiers on the hillside. For forty days, Goliath has been coming out to taunt you. You feel powerless. Then David steps forward... Goliath lies fallen... The Philistines are silenced and start to run. With your fellow-soldiers you surge forward to pursue them.

If we're like anyone in this story, it's these regular soldiers. Powerless and terrified, we see defeat turn into victory as our champion, Jesus, crushes death and the devil on our behalf. Our job now is to surge forward in the wake of Christ's triumph, to proclaim the victory he has won.

☑ Apply

❓ *When non-Christians you know think about death, how do you think they feel?*

❓ *What is their equivalent of armour and weapons—things they think may protect them, at least temporarily, from death?*

❓ *How could you use the story of David and Goliath to explain the gospel of Jesus to them?*

TIME OUT

It may seem that Saul is confused about David's identity in verses 55-58, but he already knows David. In fact he is thinking of his promise to the successful champion (v 25). Honouring the champion will involve honouring his family, especially his father.

☒ Pray

❓ *What giant problems are you facing in your life?*

❓ *What are others around you facing?*

Pray about these, reflecting on the truth that Jesus is our champion, who stands between us and evil, and who has won the decisive victory for us. Praise and worship him.

Love him or hate him

David comes to Saul's court. There are will be different responses to him, but there can be no neutral response to him.

Read 1 Samuel 18:1-30

David will replace Jonathan as the heir to the throne, yet Jonathan loves him like a brother. The phrase "one in spirit" is literally "knitted together". Jonathan makes a covenant with David (the contents of which are not specified) to express that love and trust.

> ❷ *Who else loves David (v 6-7, 16, 20, 22)? Why?*
> ❷ *How does Saul feel about this?*

In verse 10 an evil spirit comes upon Saul. "Prophesying" in 1 Samuel seems to refer to more than simply speaking God's word. It can include any effect of being overcome by a spirit, including a frenzied loss of control.

> ❷ *Does David deserve Saul's hatred? What does he say and do?*

Saul now starts to actively plot David's death. He comes up with a challenge: David can earn the right to his daughter's hand by securing the foreskins of 100 (dead) Philistines (v 24-25). David is forcibly to "convert" 100 uncircumcised Philistines whose presence defiles God's land.

The plan backfires; by the end of the chapter, David's reputation is enhanced even further, and he is part of the royal house.

☑ Apply

> ❷ *Have you ever felt usurped or been envious of another person's success?*
> ❷ *How could you make sure you don't respond like Saul?*

Three escapes

Read 1 Samuel 19:1-24

> ❷ *Who is willing to help David escape (v 1-7)?*
> ❷ *Who helps him in verses 9-17?*
> ❷ *Who helps him in verses 18-24?*

The question in verse 24 was asked once before, in 10:11. Then it was a cry of wonder and praise. This time it is a cry of scorn as Saul is totally disempowered. He is becoming a parody of his former self.

Meanwhile, David is saved by the God of Samuel: the God who rules through his word.

☑ Apply

Put yourself in the shoes of Jonathan and Michal.

> ❷ *How do these chapters describe their attitude to David?*
> ❷ *When your loyalties conflict, as theirs did, how can you decide who to follow?*
> ❷ *What can you do to display your loyalty to Jesus above all others?*

At the New Moon feast

Is it safe for David to stay in Saul's court? Jonathan thinks so. But in the course of chapter 20 he realises how wrong he is.

This is the point where Jonathan must choose between his friend and his father.

Read 1 Samuel 20:1-17

❷ *Why do you think David reminds Jonathan of the covenant they made (v 8)?*

❷ *What does Jonathan promise in response (v 9, 12-13)?*

Jonathan is yet to see the true threat to David from Saul. But he is beginning to recognise that really it is the house of Saul which is under threat from David. He sees that David will become king and triumph over his enemies (v 15), and that those enemies will include Saul. This is why he insistently makes David promise to spare him and his descendants (v 14-15, and later in v 23 and v 42).

Jonathan's choice

Read 1 Samuel 20:18-34

As agreed, Jonathan makes David's excuses. Saul's response leaves no room for doubt. He shouts that David must die.

❷ *Why does Saul say that Jonathan is acting shamefully (v 30)?*

❷ *Is he right?*

❷ *Who does Jonathan think has acted shamefully (v 34)?*

Jonathan chooses David. Now he too is the target of Saul's murderous anger (v 33; see 18:10-11; 19:9-10). And he is filled with anger himself at his father's behaviour.

Jonathan has peace with David, but at the cost of peace with Saul.

The other cost is his own status as heir to the throne. Jonathan recognises David as king. He is teaching us not just how to be a good friend of a king but—more significantly—how to be a real follower of a king.

Farewell

Read 1 Samuel 20:35-42

❷ *How is the friendship between Jonathan and David expressed in these verses?*

❷ *This time it is Jonathan who reminds David of their covenant together (v 42). Why does he do this, do you think?*

⌄ Apply

Like Jonathan, we are to give up our pretended rights to reign. We are to acclaim David's descendant Jesus as our Christ—as God's King. We are to bind our future to his and to give up control to him. By doing so, we gain a future under his protection, just as Jonathan did. Jesus says, "Whoever wants to be my disciple must deny themselves and take up their cross and follow me. For whoever wants to save their life will lose it, but whoever loses their life for me and for the gospel will save it" (Mark 8:34-35).

❷ *Are you more like Saul or more like Jonathan? How can you live more like the latter?*

True freedom

True freedom is not about being free from restraint but being set free for living rightly, in glad obedience to God's law.

Desire and response

Read Psalm 2:1-9

> ❓ What is the shared desire of the people in verses 1-3?
> ❓ What is the response (v 4-9)?

Freedom is often defined as the absence of restraint: as freedom *from* God's law (v 3). However, the universal human desire for this so-called freedom is answered in verses 4-9 by a twofold declaration.

First, God "laughs" and "scoffs" at these rebels, and says, "I have installed my king on Zion, my holy mountain" (v 6). God's king will be quite unlike the rebellious kings of verses 1-3, for he will exercise the sovereign rule of God on earth. The anointed king himself gives the second part of the declaration (v 7-9). He tells us what God in heaven has said to him: "You are my son; today *[on the day of the king's coronation/anointing]* I have become your father" (v 7).

The most important blessing that the LORD, the covenant God, gives to his anointed son, the king, is the privilege of prayer: "Ask me" (v 8). The king is invited to pray to conquer the world, to subdue all the rebellions of verses 1-3, to inherit all things, and to govern creation on behalf of God his Father. When he asks for this in prayer, his prayer will be fully granted.

⌃ Pray

> ❓ Do you see prayer as a blessing? Why / why not?
> ❓ Who could you pray for, right now, who tends to scoff at God (or at the idea of God)?

A wise kiss

Read Psalm 2:10-12

> ❓ What does wisdom look like (v 10-12)?
> ❓ How does verse 12 link back to Psalm 1 (which we looked at on 19th April).
> ❓ How is Jesus Christ, the anointed King, described in these psalms?

By the time we finish reading Psalm 2, we are (or should be) kneeling at the feet of God's anointed king, to take refuge in him from the wrath to come. The effect upon us, by the Spirit of Christ, is to subdue our proud desires for autonomy, to persuade us more deeply that Jesus really is Lord and nothing can change that, and to move us to bow the knee to him now, in this age, before it is too late.

⌃ Pray

Jesus Christ, the righteous One, is the King these psalms so beautifully and powerfully portray. Blessing is poured upon him by the Father. Blessing is to be found in him, and in him alone. Spend some time thinking about Jesus and praising him.

King in the wilderness

David is now on the run. But somehow his authority rises…

Read 1 Samuel 21:1-9 and 22:6-19

Consecrated bread was reserved for priests, but Ahimelek gave it to David. It seems from the way Jesus discusses the episode in Matthew 12:3-8 that this was because David was God's anointed one.

When Saul discovers that Ahimelek helped David, he is outraged. He enlists Doeg the Edomite—a non-Israelite—to carry out vengeance on the priests. This is a war against God. Saul is setting himself up in God's place.

Meanwhile…

Read 1 Samuel 21:10-15 (If you have time, read 21:10 – 22:23)

David heads to Gath—an odd choice, since this was Goliath's hometown.

> ❷ *How do the people of Gath view David?*
> ❷ *What is David's strategy for escape?*

David reflects on this episode in Psalms 34 and 56. There, he attributes his escape to God: "This poor man called, and the LORD heard him; he saved him out of all his troubles … Taste and see that the LORD is good; blessed is the one who takes refuge in him" (Psalm 34:6, 8).

This is proved true in the cave of Adullam, where David's kingdom begins to take shape. This is an alternative Israel in the making, featuring a king, a prophet (1 Samuel 22:5) and a priest (v 20).

On the margins

Read 1 Samuel 23:1-25

> ❷ *What is David's leadership like?*
> ❷ *How do we know God is on his side (v 4-5, 10-12)?*
> ❷ *Why do you think the local people are so ready to betray him (v 12, 19-20)?*
> ❷ *How do you think David feels during this chapter?*

Verse 18 is rather poignant: Jonathan goes home, but David has no home to go to. He is in the wilderness, on the margins, both literally and metaphorically.

If this is how Israel's greatest king came to his throne, then it should be no surprise that this was also how Israel's ultimate King, Jesus, came to his throne.

⌃ Pray

Followers of Christ can expect to suffer and be mistreated, too. "We must go through many hardships to enter the kingdom of God" (Acts 14:22). We can respond to suffering with faith, knowing that our road ultimately leads to the kingdom.

Read through Psalm 34 and use it to inform your prayers for yourself and for those you know who are suffering.

Strength like no other

What comfort could anyone possibly give David in the wilderness?

Finding strength
Read 1 Samuel 23:15-18

Jonathan comes specifically to provide comfort to David. He doesn't say, *Things aren't so bad*, or *Maybe it'll be better soon*. No—he helps him to find strength in God, reminding him that his kingdom will be established by God. This is exactly the encouragement David needs.

On the rock
Read 1 Samuel 23:26-29

David and Saul are on opposite sides of a mountain, which is referred to in Hebrew simply as "the rock". This rock protects David by keeping him apart from his enemy.

At the end of his life, David was to say, "The LORD is my rock" (2 Samuel 22:2). He realised that all along God had been like that rock. He stands between us and our enemies, between us and death. God is our refuge in times of trouble.

In the cave
Read 1 Samuel 24:1-22

David is conscience-stricken about cutting Saul's robe because this symbolises tearing the kingdom away from him (see 15:27-28). David doesn't want to grab the kingdom.

> ❓ What does he do with the piece of fabric (24:11)?

> ❓ What are his reasons for sparing Saul (v 6, 10-12)?
> ❓ What hopes does he express for the future (v 12, 15)?

Saul is contrite—at least for now. He acknowledges that David will succeed him as king and, like Jonathan, asks David to swear not to wipe out his family or his name.

> ❓ Where in this chapter can you see that David's strength is in God?

Fast-forward

In the cave, David had the opportunity to skip his life of suffering and fast-forward to the throne. But that is not God's way. It was not God's plan. So it was not David's.

We too cannot skip suffering. That way does not really lead to glory. Instead we need to find strength in God, having confidence in God's way of doing things, and trusting that Christ's kingdom will be established in the end.

⌄ Apply

> ❓ How do you tend to comfort suffering friends? How could you help them find strength in God?
> ❓ In your life, how has God taught or shaped you through suffering?
> ❓ If you are suffering now, what could God be teaching you through it? How could you learn from David's example?

It is mine to avenge

David faces two more tests. Will he trust the Lord and act with justice?

David and his men have been protecting the flocks of a wealthy man called Nabal. Now they ask him to be generous to them in recognition of their services.

Read 1 Samuel 25:1-17, 23-35 (If you have time, read 25:1-44)

> ❷ *How does Nabal view David (v 10-11)?*
> ❷ *How does his servant view David (v 15-16)?*
> ❷ *What does David decide to do (v 21-22)?*
> ❷ *What is Abigail's attitude to David (v 23-31)?*

Abigail reminds David that he spared Saul (v 26) and urges him to do the same for Nabal (v 25, 31). Taking vengeance will make David guilty, however just it seems to him. She repeatedly tells him that God is the one who will protect him and deal with his enemies.

> ❷ *How does David respond (v 32-35)?*
> ❷ *How does he interpret what happens to Nabal (v 39)?*

Guiltless

Read 1 Samuel 26:1-12

Once again David is betrayed and pursued. But somehow he has the upper hand.

> ❷ *What does David find when he arrives in the camp (v 7)?*
> ❷ *How would you have interpreted the scene?*

Unlike in chapter 24, David does not even consider killing Saul. He's learned from Abigail and is content for God to be the judge.

Paul commends the same attitude to those who are in Christ: "Do not take revenge, my dear friends, but leave room for God's wrath, for it is written: 'It is mine to avenge; I will repay,' says the Lord" (Romans 12:19). Caring about justice means acting in obedience to God rather than out of a desire to vindicate or avenge ourselves.

Read 1 Samuel 26:13-25

> ❷ *How does David describe the way he has been treated (v 18-20)?*
> ❷ *How does he describe his own actions (v 23-24)?*
> ❷ *What links are there with Jesus here?*

Saul admits, "Surely I have acted like a fool"—just like Nabal (25:25). But David is not a fool; he will not grasp his kingdom through bloodshed.

⌃ Pray

We often suggest to God how he might, or even should, act. But he understands things far better than we do. When everything seems to be going wrong, we need to have faith that God will establish his kingdom.

Pray about any difficult or painful situations in your life. Ask God to help you act with righteousness and faithfulness (26:23). Ask him for the gift of faith, and for wise friends like Abigail to remind you of God's way.

What should I do?

None of us want to do the wrong thing. But how do we figure out what that is?

In exile

Scan-read 1 Samuel 27:1 – 28:2

Previously David was desperate to remain in Israel (26:20), but now he gives up on that.

> ❓ *What does David say to himself (27:1)? How is this different from what he said in the previous chapter?*

The writer's concern isn't to judge David's morality but to present the purposes and promises of God, and how people respond. God is not mentioned in this chapter, so we can't draw firm conclusions about whether David is right to do what he does next.

David enters the employ of the Philistine king. He conducts raids on the traditional enemies of God's people but tells Achish that he is raiding Israel.

> ❓ *What cliffhanger does the writer leave us on (28:1-2)?*

In Endor

Read 1 Samuel 28:3-25

The writer switches our attention back to Saul. Saul is terrified by the advancing Philistine army. He wants a word from God, but God is silent. Unlike with David, this time it is clear that we are not to approve Saul's actions.

> ❓ *How does the writer emphasise the fact that Saul is breaking the law (v 8-10)?*

> ❓ *Why is he doing so?*
> ❓ *Why do people visit mediums or attend spiritualist churches today? What are they seeking?*

Many spiritualists are charlatans. But some are not. The Bible tells us that the spiritual world does exist. However, if encounters with spirits are real, they are not with the dead but with evil spirits. Leviticus 19:31 prohibits consulting mediums because it defiles you: it involves things which are not of God and which try to replace God. 1 Corinthians 10:19-20 says demons are behind pagan worship.

At Endor God does allow someone to appear from the dead. But Saul meets with no word of reassurance. Samuel repeats the word of judgment that he has spoken before.

▼ Apply

> ❓ *How could you use this story to talk about spiritualism with friends who are attracted by it?*

Read 1 John 4:1-6

> ❓ *How can you know whether someone's advice or lifestyle is of God or not (v 1-3)?*
> ❓ *Think about where else you tend to seek guidance or reassurance. Is that of God?*
> ❓ *How can you seek God's presence and God's wisdom in the Bible?*

Full circle

The final chapters of 1 Samuel bring us to a familiar scenario.

❓ *What was the cliffhanger when we left David in 1 Samuel 28:1-2?*

Read 1 Samuel 29:1-11

❓ *How is the cliffhanger resolved?*

In verse 8 David keeps up the pretence and feigns disappointment. But he must surely have been mightily relieved. He had been in a fix, and now he was given a way out. His words are ambiguous: "Why can't I go and fight against the enemies of my lord the king?" The question is, who does David consider to be his king?

David rises

Read 1 Samuel 30:1-6, 18-25 (If you have time, read 30:1-31)

❓ *How does David feel when he gets back to Ziklag (v 4, 6)? Why?*

Where David's strength fails (v 4), God's strength takes over (v 6). David turns to the Lord for guidance and is promised success. Over the next verses there is a total turnaround. The men who threatened David before (v 6) now proclaim, "This is David's plunder" (v 20).

❓ *How is David like a king in verses 21-25?*
❓ *What kind of king is he?*

Samuel had warned that a king would take, take, take (8:10-18); but David gives, gives, gives. He gives to the men who fought with him, he gives to the ones left behind, and finally he gives to the leaders of Judah.

❓ *How does this episode in chapter 30 put David in a position of strength?*

Saul falls

Read 1 Samuel 31:1-13

❓ *How do the Philistines win the battle?*
❓ *Who kills Saul (v 4)?*
❓ *How are Saul's fears in verse 4 confirmed (v 9-10)?*

The book ends where it began, with the Philistines winning a victory and the death of Israel's leader along with his sons.

Two kings

There have been two kings in Israel, with two kingdoms, two courts and two armies. One is on a downward trajectory that ends with his fall on the battlefield. The other is on an upward trajectory that will end with his enthronement as king.

In the world today there are also two kingdoms—the kingdom of Christ and the kingdom of this world. Only one of these— only Christ's kingdom—will triumph.

⬆ Pray

1 Samuel 31 is a sober ending to the book. Reflecting on this, pray for people you know who do not yet know Christ or put their trust in his kingdom.

Bible in a year: Numbers 9-11 • Revelation 18

David and Jesus

How would you sum up the message of 1 Samuel? There's time for one last look at the story of Israel's first kings.

The final chapters of 1 Samuel focus on the conflict between Saul and David, but it is important to recognise the trajectory of the whole book. It is not from Saul to David but from no monarchy to monarchy. The book starts with a barren woman who speaks of a coming king (1 Samuel 2:10).

We are presented with three options:

1. No rule or self-rule (Judges 21:25)

2. Rule through a human king—a king like those of the nations

3. God's rule through God's king

Is monarchy really a good thing for Israel? The answer appears to be, *Yes, when you have a good king ruling under God's kingship.*

The greatest king

In the book of 2 Samuel, David will become king over Israel, and God will make a covenant with him.

Read 2 Samuel 7:8-16

> ❷ *What does God highlight about David's origins (v 8)?*
> ❷ *How has God acted as David's king?*
> ❷ *What does he promise for the future?*

David's promised greater son is Jesus. Like David, he is an unlikely king, coming from the margins. But he is the one who fully represents God's rule on earth, and his kingdom lasts for ever.

Our options

"Israel had no king; everyone did as they saw fit." (Judges 21:25)

"We want a king over us. Then we shall be like all the other nations, with a king to lead us and to go out before us and fight our battles." (1 Samuel 8:19-20)

> ❷ *Are there times when you long to rule yourself, doing as you see fit?*
> ❷ *Are there times when you seek authority and protection from others?*
> ❷ *What is the third option?*

⌄ Apply

> ❷ *If someone said to you, "We should all do whatever is right for us personally", how would you respond?*
> ❷ *What about if someone said, "I want someone to look after me and help me know what to do"?*
> ❷ *How could you use the story of 1 Samuel to respond to those statements?*

⌃ Pray

Look back at Hannah's prayer in 2:1-10. Think about how it has been fulfilled in the course of 1 Samuel. Consider what it means for your own life and for the world today. Then use it as your own prayer.

A bird in the storm

You watch a coastal bird in a storm as it flies up to some clifftop cleft in the rocks and hides there, completely safe. That's the image at the start of Psalm 11.

Read Psalm 11:1-3

❷ *What is David being urged to do (v 1), and why (v 2-3)?*

❷ *In verse 2, what people, preparation, action and target do we hear of?*

"The wicked" means people who set themselves and their whole direction of life against God. Their *preparation* is described in the vivid language of archers getting ready to fire deadly arrows. Their *action* is "to shoot from the shadows". This is not open warfare; this is an ambush. And their *target* is "the upright in heart": those whose determination is to act rightly before God.

When Bible poetry speaks of "the foundations" (v 3), it means the moral foundations of society. All around David the king and those who stand with him, the moral order of the world is collapsing. There is, it seems, nothing that he or they can do.

Today, we see the media promote "freedom" and "tolerance" rather than God's good law. Church-attendance statistics show that believers are getting older and that fewer young people are trusting Christ as Lord. You may even have experienced moral corruption in your own church.

❷ *How do these things make you feel?*

❷ *How would you like to respond to them?*

God is on his throne

We need the rest of the psalm to see why we can take refuge in God and persevere with the work of our King and his gospel.

Read Psalm 11:4-7

❷ *Why can the king, and the king's people, safely make God their refuge?*

❷ *In contrast, what awaits the wicked?*

We shy away from the strong language in verses 5-6, but God in heaven hates the wicked. They are "those who love violence", who are actively plotting against God's king and his people (v 2). God is passionately against them—those who destroy the moral foundations of society will themselves be suddenly and finally destroyed.

❷ *How do these truths make you feel?*

❷ *How will they help you to live positively and publicly as a Christian this week?*

Jesus sings

Jesus, our King, when he sang this psalm, pledged to entrust himself to the Father and not to abandon his task as King. He determined to walk the whole path of suffering to accomplish it, until he could cry, "It is finished!" (John 19:30)—and then enter into his kingdom with joy. The truly wonderful thing is this: we who appropriate this promise are by nature wicked. Only because our King took upon himself our punishment can we hope to stand before God on the last day. Because our King stands before the Father, so shall we! *Praise him now!*

1 JOHN: Gospel freedom

In John's day there were people who said that Jesus was not both God and man. The same is true today. John's letter wants to get us straight on the basics, so that we can be sure.

What you should feel

Read 1 John 1:1-4

- ❓ *John's opening words seem a little cryptic. What is he saying, do you think?*
- ❓ *Why might he need to emphasise this?*
- ❓ *What should we feel at the end of reading this letter (v 4)?*

Today people are more likely to say that Jesus was really just a man who taught us *about* God or gave us some insight into God. In John's day, it seems to have been the opposite. The Greek world thought flesh was dirty or corrupt, and so they could not get their heads around the idea that Jesus was God *incarnate*. John tells them in plain language, *We saw him, heard him, touched him.* Jesus, the Word of life, who lived with the Father, appeared in human flesh. Grasping this truth is vital because it is intimately connected to experiencing the truth of the gospel—to enjoying fellowship with God and being joined to his people. It's only when we embrace this truth that our joy will be complete (v 4): full and never-ending.

⌄ Apply

False teaching will often come down to this: Jesus was not both fully God and fully man. Ask a Jehovah's Witness or a Mormon, (and sadly, many members and leaders in mainline churches) and you will discover that this life-draining, Bible-denying, joy-sapping heresy is alive and well in our generation. We must be aware of it and sure of our ground to oppose it and to defend the truth; because only the truth about Christ can bring real life to people.

- ❓ *Which are you most likely to tip over into: forgetting that Jesus is really God or forgetting that he is really man?*

A message that matters

Read 1 John 1:5-7

- ❓ *What lie is John talking about here? Why is this lie an attractive one to believe?*
- ❓ *What is the test for whether our walk with Christ is genuine or not? What do you think this means?*
- ❓ *What benefits do we experience when we walk in the light (v 7)?*

Light and darkness simply do not mix. So don't think you can know God and continue to live your way. How can you expect to be friends with God and rebel against him at the same time?! Notice that this is the message of Jesus himself (v 5); how we live really matters and is the test of whether or not our faith is genuine. Living in the light is striving to be holy as we please God—and as we do so, we can be confident of forgiveness through Jesus and enjoy a genuine connection with his family.

⌃ Pray

Thank God for the gospel of light; and pray you would make a genuine response to it.

Freely forgiven

John is addressing two opposite errors: first, that you can know God and still walk in darkness; second, that you do not sin and therefore do not need God's forgiveness.

Both of these views are alive and well today.

❓ *Have you heard or seen these two views expressed? What form did they take?*

❓ *Which of these two false views are you most prone to believing (and living)?*

Self deceit

Read 1 John 1:8-10

These are glorious verses, often used in church liturgies before a prayer of confession. Let's think carefully about them.

❓ *How easy is it, do you think, to deceive ourselves about just how sinful we are?*

❓ *Why would we think that way?*

❓ *What is the first step in the remedy for this false thinking?*

It might be our pride, a sense of our own guilt, or the result of comparing ourselves with others who we think we are "better" than. Whatever the cause, claiming to be without sin is self-deceit and a denial of the gospel truth about ourselves. *You and I are sinners.* And the first step towards finding forgiveness is to recognise that—to confess our sins, not just in a general sense but in specific detail (v 9).

Wonderful grace

Re-read 1 John 1:8-10

❓ *Why does John also say that God is just, do you think?*

❓ *What two things does God offer to those who come to him knowing that they are unworthy sinners deserving of judgment?*

God is faithful (v 9) to his promises and to his wayward people. But perhaps supremely, he is faithful to the willing sacrifice of his Son, the Lord Jesus. At the cross, both justice and mercy were satisfied. Not only does God's grace forgive us, but it works in us to "purify us from all sin"—the lifelong process of walking away from sin towards a life of righteous holiness.

Undeniable realities

❓ *What conclusion do these verses tell us we should draw if someone denies the reality of sin?*

▽ Apply

People tend to hate the idea of sin! It is seen as old-fashioned, repressive, guilt-inducing, and destructive—especially if we dare say that children are sinners! And yet these claims fly in the face of God's word, our own experience and common sense. God does not lie about this painful truth because he loves us and wants us to know the joy and freedom that forgiveness brings.

❓ *What will it mean for you to take these verses seriously in your view of your own life, your prayers to God, and your words to others?*

Free to sin?

John uses the language of opposites to press his point home—light and darkness, truth and lies, love and hate—but his purpose is to help us see the issues at stake.

What grace has done
Read 1 John 2:1-6

❓ *Do you think it is possible not to sin and to "live as Jesus did" (v 1, 6)?*

❓ *What two wonderful truths about Jesus does John lay out for us in verses 1-2?*

❓ *Why do we need both?*

John is aiming these words at two different sorts of people: *the complacent,* who think that because God forgives them, it doesn't matter how they live; and *the fearful,* who think that because they sin, they cannot truly know God. John's concern is to reassure the fearful without making the complacent more complacent; and to challenge the complacent without making the fearful even less assured. The answer for both is to understand the work of Jesus, both on the cross *then* and in heaven *now.*

First, Jesus was an atoning sacrifice *then* on the cross. Literally, Jesus is the "propitiation for our sins"—his death satisfies and turns away God's wrath from us.

Second, Jesus is also an advocate for us *now.* Imagine you're standing before a king, trying to explain your rebellion against him—and then the king's own son steps forward and speaks on your behalf. Or imagine a law court in which you're in the dock, and there's no doubt you're guilty—but then your lawyer plays his trump card: an argument no one can refute. He has already paid the penalty for your crime in full. Jesus is that advocate for us before the Father now.

Responding to grace
Re-read 1 John 2:1-6

❓ *How do we know that our faith is genuine, and that we have truly been forgiven (v 3-6)?*

❓ *What does it mean to "love ... God" in these verses (v 5)?*

⌄ Apply

When we truly love someone, it is more than a feeling; we will genuinely want to please them, and we will change in order to do so. And we will want to grow like them in the things we admire about them. It is the same for true believers in Christ. It might seem that we can grab his forgiveness and then carry on as normal. But the sign that we have truly understood the gospel message is that it is changing us. It's a hard test to apply to ourselves, and even harder to others. But the important thing is not so much how obviously sinful or holy you are, but rather your direction of travel: towards love and purity, and away from sin and pride. That is true love for God.

❓ *Looking at yourself, how do you stack up against this test?*

❓ *If you fear you do not come out very well, what does 1:9 and 2:1-2 encourage you to do and to know?*

Free to love

At first, John seems to be a little confused in this passage. Is what he is talking about new or isn't it?

Old yet new
Read 1 John 2:7-11

> ❷ *What new "faith test" does John give us in verse 10?*
> ❷ *How is this both an old and a new commandment, do you think?*

In verses 3-5, John has been saying that we must walk our talk. The sign of being a Christian is obedience. Now he imagines someone responding, *Hang on a minute— when I signed up to Christianity, I was told it was all about grace and mercy: that it wasn't what I did that counted but what God had done for me. Now you're springing something new on us.*

So John reminds his readers that obedience has always been the sign of belonging to God's people. It is nothing new. The gospel calls us to faith and to repentance—turning from sin to obey God. It was the message of the Old Testament and the message that Jesus preached (Micah 6:8; Mark 1:14-15).

☑ Apply

> ❷ *Is the call to repentance and obedience part of the way you present the gospel to others?*
> ❷ *What happens when it gets left out?*
> ❷ *How can we talk about repentance and the obedience of faith without giving someone the impression that we in some way earn salvation?*

For the old and young
Read 1 John 2:12-14

In these verses, the style suddenly changes, and the repeated phrase "I am writing to you..." shows us that John is summarising what he has said so far in his letter.

> ❷ *What three important points does John want to impress upon us all?*
> ❷ *Who is "him who is from the beginning" (v 13, 14)?*
> ❷ *What new perspective does John introduce in the last line of verse 14?*

His summary is simply this: we are sinners, God forgives us through Jesus, and because of this, we should strive to live a sin-free life. This is the message as it has *always* been, because it is the message of the Father and Son, who are from the beginning. But this life is also new, because it is the life that shows we are part of the new age that Jesus ushered in. Love towards God and other believers is characteristic of the new age of light, which has overcome the kingdom of darkness, the kingdom of Satan.

☐ Pray

Thank God that you can be part of this new era through the cross of Christ.

And ask God to help you walk in the right direction: to live like Christ and to overcome the evil one.

Free to be different

Christians belong to the dawning new age of the rule of King Jesus. But for the time being, we still have to live in the real world of rebellion and hatred.

It's a tension with which we all struggle.

For God so loved…
Read 1 John 2:15

❓ *What are we being called to do in this verse?*

❓ *How does this square with what is said about "the world" in John 3:16, do you think?*

The word "world" in the Bible can be used in very different ways. (The seventeenth-century theologian John Owen listed no fewer than 16 different nuances of it!) It can simply refer to everything that God has made—the planet we live on and the people who live on it. John 3:16 tells us that God loved the rebellious people he made so much he sent his own Son to die. But in this letter, "the world" is shorthand for the way of thinking and living that dominates a world that is hostile to God—and all social and cultural pressures on believers to conform to those sinful patterns of behaviour. God hates this sinful way of life—and he expects us to hate it too—even when we see it in ourselves.

Rejecting the world
Read 1 John 2:16-29

❓ *What three characteristics of worldly thinking and living does John point out for us in verse 16?*

❓ *Struggling against the world is hard, so why bother (v 17, 27)?*

❓ *What else will make it difficult for us to live in this world (v 18-19)?*

❓ *What does John encourage us to do as we face this hostility (v 28)?*

❓ *What have we been given to help us with this (v 20, 21)?*

The pressure of sin is everywhere. From within ourselves (the lust of the flesh, v 16), from outside (the lust of the eyes) and from the arrogant pride in ourselves that defaults to boasting about ourselves with no dependence on God or gratitude towards him. But these are all part of a world that is dead and passing away (v 17). Those who truly belong to Christ have received the truth about him, have been anointed by the Holy Spirit and have the sure hope of eternity to look forward to. John encourages us to "continue in him" as we reject false teachers and the pull of worldly sinfulness. We walk away from these things towards the goodness and light of God's new creation.

❓ *How do we recognise antichrists (v 22)?*

❓ *Why can it sometimes be difficult to spot them (v 21)?*

❓ *What do you think it means in practice to "continue in him" (v 28)?*

⌃ Pray

Turn your answers to the questions above into prayers.

Free to obey

"He's got his mother's eyes... I'm afraid she's going to have her father's nose... She looks just like her Great-aunt Mabel..."

We all know the routine. Everyone coos over the newborn, trying to work out who they resemble, when all the time they look like... well... like a baby! John says we have become God's children. The question is: do we show the family likeness?

What we are and will be
Read 1 John 3:1-3

> ❷ List out the things that show how God has lavished his love on us.
> ❷ What can we look forward to?
> ❷ What should knowing this cause us to do now?

TIME OUT

The language is so familiar to us that it's easy not to be amazed by it. John, however, half expects his readers not to believe it, so he adds, "And that is what we are!" Take time to reflect on the lavish love of God. You might find it helpful to meditate on these verses: **1 John 4:9-10; John 13:1-17; Romans 8:31-39.**

Even John acknowledges that precisely what will happen to us in the new creation is a bit of a mystery (1 John 3:2). We don't know what we will be like when Christ returns and we are transformed. But John *does* know that we will be like Jesus and we will see Jesus as he really is—the glorious Lord over all creation.

In the meantime, out of gratitude for the love God has lavished upon us, our goal should be to bridge the gap. With the certain hope of one day being pure like Christ, we try to purify ourselves now. John knows we can't be sinless yet (see 1:8). But he expects us to try as hard as we can to become as pure as we can.

What sin really is
Read 1 John 3:4-6

> ❷ How does verse 4 make sin so much bigger than simply law-breaking?
> ❷ Why will true Christians not keep on habitually sinning in the same way again and again (v 5-6)?

Sin is not just rule-breaking; it is a rejection of the rule-giver: God. It's not simply that I know a law but fail to keep it. Sin's essence—"lawlessness"—is that we make ourselves the arbiters of the law, deciding whether or not we will keep it. You can be a lawless lawkeeper! And that's why we need the new hearts that God gives us when we trust in Christ and as he pours out his Spirit on us. We've been born of God. We have God's genes, and so we *cannot* go on sinning. But we need a constant reminder of this in the face of the pressure of the world and our own sinful nature.

Pray

Think of a couple of specific ways you want to grow more like Jesus. Then speak to God about them—today, and every day.

Prayers and answers

By nature we long for our own success, safety or comfort. The challenge from Psalm 20 is to root our deepest desires in the victory of our King instead.

❓ *Think back to your prayers over the past two days. What were they about?*

In Psalm 20, the people pray for their king.

The people pray
Read Psalm 20:1-9

❓ *What do the people pray on behalf of their king?*
❓ *What title for God is used four times in this psalm?*

The psalm is opened up if we look for the word "answer". In verse 1 the people pray that the LORD will "answer" the king. All of verses 1-5 are a prayer that the king's prayers will be answered. The covenant God (the LORD) is the One who protected Jacob when he was in distress (see Genesis 35:3—"God, who answered me in the day of my distress"). The God of Jacob is the LORD who will answer his king when he, too, is in deep distress (Psalm 20:1).

Read Psalm 20:4 again

❓ *What do these desires and plans need to be, if God is going to answer this prayer?*

The prayer in verse 4 is that God will give the king the desires of his heart and make all his plans succeed. The king's heart and affections are to be so aligned with the purposes of God that they will all be granted, because they are precisely in tune with the will of God.

We can pray this too, because we know the only king who has ever fulfilled this description: Jesus. Our King is not a cardboard cutout; he has desires in his heart; he makes plans and wants them to succeed. When we pray this psalm, we ask God in heaven to give Jesus, our King, what he deeply desires.

The Lord answers
Re-read Psalm 20:6-9

❓ *What do we learn about the LORD, the covenant God, from these verses?*
❓ *How do verses 6-9 prove that God can answer the prayers in verses 1-5?*

A leader of the people leads them in confident assurance that what they have asked for in verses 1-5 will indeed be granted. The prayers of their king will be answered. The speaker is sure, and assures us, that "the LORD gives victory to his anointed" (v 6).

☑ Apply

I can want success for myself as much as I like, but I cannot be sure of getting it. But when I want Jesus to succeed, my longings will be granted.

❓ *How will this psalm reshape your desires so that you begin genuinely to care more about the victories of King Jesus than about your own success or failure?*

🔽 *Bible in a year: Numbers 35-36 • Matthew 5 v 1-26*

Free to follow

You cannot continue to sin? But hang on, we want to say, hasn't John already established that each us of does sin? And isn't that our daily experience?

He breaks the power

Read 1 John 3:7-10

- ❓ *What simple equation does John want us to understand from verses 7-8 and 10?*
- ❓ *What does it mean that someone is "of the devil", do you think?*
- ❓ *Why did Jesus come (v 8)?*

In one sense it is inevitable that we will sin. But in another sense it's not. Jesus has destroyed the work of the devil. The power and penalty of sin are broken, even if we still live with its presence. So we don't have any excuse. We can't give up the struggle against sin because we think that it's inevitable that we succumb to it. The tempter still tempts, but he can be resisted. John is saying that in general terms believers will think and do right, and unbelievers will not.

✔ Apply

- ❓ *Is there something wrong that you keep on doing?*

Don't despair! Every Christian sins, but a true Christian can't go on sinning without being concerned—without struggling to be right. So to struggle with sin is not a sign of unbelief but a sign of true life. Most unbelievers couldn't care less whether they sin or not. Only a true child of God struggles against sin, confesses their sin, and enjoys knowing they are forgiven of their sin.

Talk to the Lord about that now.

Murder in church

Read 1 John 3:11-15

- ❓ *Why does John quote the example of Cain and Abel? What does it illustrate?*
- ❓ *What are we told we should expect if we are living for God?*
- ❓ *Why is it so vital to love one another?*

Cain's hatred came to a climax in murder. Of course, few of us go that far. But before we let ourselves off the hook, John says that anyone who hates his brother is just as bad as a murderer! The difference is in degree, not in nature. This teaching comes straight from the lips of the Lord Jesus (see Matthew 5:21-24). Those who love Christ are our family and our future. Loving our brothers and sisters is a mark that we truly belong to the family and have the same shared future.

And don't be surprised if people hate you because you're a Christian. Cain hated Abel because Abel was righteous. Now that you've been made right with God, people will hate us in the same way. After all, the world hated Jesus (John 15:18-21).

⌃ Pray

Pray that God would give you a deep, passionate and sincere love for your brothers and sisters in Christ. Ask him to make you willing to suffer rejection for your faith, and to give you the joy that comes from knowing you're following in the steps of your Master.

Free from guilt

According to my dictionary, love is "warm affection, attachment, liking, or fondness, paternal benevolence, affectionate devotion". Not bad, but not good enough for John.

Real love
Read 1 John 3:16-18

- ❷ *Where does John point our attention so that we can see what real love is?*
- ❷ *So what kind of love should Christians be showing to others?*

Real love is seen in costly, practical action—and so real love is seen supremely at the cross. Intentions and warm feelings towards others are good, but only if they result in practical action—in doing something. Talk is cheap unless it is accompanied by deeds.

⌄ Apply

A third of the world does not have access to basic sanitation. Hundreds of millions of Christians are not able to get an education. Many are persecuted because of their faith. What are you doing for your brothers and sisters in need? John isn't interested in words—he's after practical action (v 18).

- ❷ *So what are you going to do about it?*

Real peace
Read 1 John 3:19-24

- ❷ *What should we do if our hearts condemn us before God (v 20)?*
- ❷ *What happens if our hearts do not condemn us before God (v 21)?*
- ❷ *What do you make of verse 22?*

Conscience is that God-given sense that tells us that what we're doing is right or wrong. But sin has messed it up. Some people's consciences are almost dead, while others have hearts that condemn them unnecessarily. In the latter case, we look at our lives and wonder how we have the nerve to call ourselves Christians when we are so sinful. John reminds us that Jesus has delivered us from condemnation through his death in our place.

Our love for others is one reassuring sign of his work in us. But at the end of the day, it is God who reassures us. He is greater than our hearts (v 20). Christ bore our judgment on the cross. The answer to a condemning heart is the gospel—the message of freedom and forgiveness through Jesus Christ.

And when we truly understand that we are accepted by God through Christ, we can stand confidently in his presence and ask boldly. God gives us what we want when we want what God wants (v 22). So ask away for what pleases God—especially that your friends, family and neighbours would believe in the name of his Son (v 23).

⌃ Pray

Use verse 23 as a basis for prayer. Pray for all those you normally pray for (including yourself), and some whom you don't pray for. Ask God to grow their faith in his Son and their love for others.

Free to overcome

Spirituality is far more popular than religion these days. And we tend to see what is "spiritual" as by definition good. John does not agree...

Test the spirits

Read 1 John 4:1-3

> ❷ *What are the "spirits" that John says we should test (v 1)?*
> ❷ *What test should we apply?*

Whether it's teaching, prophecy, a new spirituality or whatever, the key issue is Jesus. How does this "spirit" answer these kinds of questions: Is he the Son of God? Is he fully human? Is he the only Saviour? Is his work sufficient to save us? Did he die as our substitute? Is he unique? Is he the King? Will he judge the world?

▼ Apply

In John's day, the main issue was whether Jesus came "in the flesh"—was Jesus really fully human (see 1:1-3)? The issue will vary from one generation to another, but always it will be about who Jesus is and what he has done.

> ❷ *What do you think the issues are for us?*

Oppose the spirits

Read 1 John 4:4-6

> ❷ *What great truth in verse 4 helps us in our battle against these various spirits?*
> ❷ *Who listens to whom, according to verses 5-6? How is this both an explanation and a challenge for us as we seek to share the truth with others?*

Whether "the spirits" are demonic forces or alternative spiritualities or worldly viewpoints, we have already overcome them. We don't need to fear them or their arguments because God is greater. Verse 6 might sound arrogant at first glance, but John is talking about the apostolic testimony to Jesus—"what we have seen and heard" (1:3). It is a further refinement of his truth test. There are many different versions of who Jesus is and what he has done, but the only version that counts is the apostolic one, which we have in the New Testament. After all, the apostles were there. They saw Jesus and they heard him for themselves.

It is not arrogant to claim that we know the truth. It is not arrogant to say that other people are wrong. We don't know the truth because we were clever enough to figure it out or good enough to attain it, but because God was gracious enough to reveal it to us.

⌃ Pray

> ❷ *Are you ever frightened to speak out and put a Christian point of view? Do you worry that you'll be laughed at or argued down?*

Remember that the One who is in you is greater than the one who is in the world.

Pray for opportunities to humbly and gently but confidently tell others about the real Jesus, who can rescue us from our sins for a glorious future.

Free to love others

John has been talking about a truth test—we can test the spirits by what they make of Jesus. Now he talks about a love test.

God is love
Read 1 John 4:7-8

❓ *Where does love come from?*

❓ *Is John saying that people who aren't Christians cannot love? If not, then what is he saying, do you think?*

❓ *What is the difference between saying "God loves" and "God is love"?*

God is *always* loving. Everything he does is characterised by love. He doesn't act in love sometimes and in wrath at other times. So even when he is acting in judgment, it is a loving act. When God judges sin in sinners, he is showing that he loves those that their sin has hurt, and loving the world he has made. He doesn't have a split personality or changeable moods. All his actions have complete integrity with every part of his character. He never compromises his love for the sake of his holiness or his justice for the sake of his love.

By God's common grace, non-Christians can be loving, sacrificial and generous— sometimes more so than some who would call themselves Christians. But they will never love God's people or God himself in the same way that those who truly belong to him do.

The love test
Read 1 John 4:7-12

❓ *How would you summarise the love test from these verses?*

No one has ever seen God, John says (v 12).

❓ *But in what two places can people see God's love?*

❓ *What does this tell us about our priorities as Christians?*

God is love, and love comes from God. So if we claim to be born of God, then we must be characterised by the kind of sacrificial love that we were shown at the cross. God's love has a purpose for us—eternal life. And it didn't wait for someone else to make the first move.

We see God's love at the cross. But we can also experience it in the fellowship of the church family (v 12). That's why the quality of our life together as Christians is so vital if we are to bring the forgiveness and mercy of God to those who are lost without him.

🔼 Pray

Pray that people will be able to see God and his love in the relationships that you have with one another in your church.

Free to believe

John tells us that the Spirit gives us confidence in the gospel and in our salvation. But how can we know whether our faith is the real thing?

Truth plus love…

Read 1 John 4:13-21

- ❓ *How do we know that we live in God and that he lives in us (v 13)?*
- ❓ *And how do we know that the Spirit lives in us (v 14-21)?*
- ❓ *What does it mean to "rely" on the love of God, do you think (v 16a)?*

It should come as no surprise to us that these are not separate tests, as though we can get some right and others wrong. They are all part and parcel of the same thing. The sign that we have truly been given the Spirit is that we "testify that the Father has sent the Son to be the Saviour of the world" (v 14) and that Jesus is God's Son (v 15). But acknowledging the truth isn't enough. The truth must also make a difference in our lives. It's not that we attract God's love by being loving. Quite the opposite—we love because he first loved us. Our love is the fruit of his love at work in our lives.

Many people pit "spirituality", "love" and "truth" against one another. Doctrine divides while love unites, some say. Other churches are strong on spirituality but weak on truth, we might say. But such divisions don't make sense to John. And that's because his definition of love is the same as his definition of truth. Neither can be real unless they come together, from the indwelling Spirit. This is the only true "spirituality" that counts.

✅ Apply

- ❓ *Do you ever treat love and truth as alternatives? What about your church?*
- ❓ *How would you push back at a brother or sister who makes a comment that pits these qualities against each other?*

… equals confidence

Re-read 1 John 4:16-18

- ❓ *Who might we be fearful of, and why (v 17-18)?*
- ❓ *What link is John drawing between love and this kind of fear (v 18b)?*

Without Christ we would still fear the day of judgment. It would rightly terrify us. But God's love for us means we can have confidence—confidence that on the day of judgment we will be acquitted. If we are still unsure about the completeness and finality of our forgiveness in Christ, it will compromise our love for God, and our ability to enjoy everything Christ has given to us.

⌃ Pray

Are you confident that the day of judgment holds no terror for you—because of Christ? If so, give thanks and approach his throne with confidence in your prayers.

If not, read 1 John 1:8-9 again, and ask God's Spirit to give you reassurance.

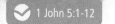

Truth, love and obedience

John seems to be repeating himself—going round and round in circles. But that's the whole point. Truth, love and obedience all lead to each other and all belong together.

A virtuous circle

Read 1 John 5:1-5

❓ *Try to draw a diagram of how each of the things John mentions leads to the next thing. (Hint: It's a circle!)*

John says that the commands of God are not burdensome (v 3).

❓ *What commands is he talking about?*
❓ *Why are they not burdensome?*
❓ *Why do we feel they can be sometimes?*
❓ *Is it God or our faith that has overcome the world (v 4-5)?*

We may struggle with God's command to love others and to speak the gospel to those who are hostile, but neither command is burdensome in the sense of being too big for us or an irrelevant thing to do. God has been victorious over the world and the devil at the cross of Christ. It's a victory we can share in and get a taste of as we put our trust in him. We may feel that our lives are a series of difficult skirmishes and battles that we mostly lose, but the truth is that, in Christ, we are victorious. It's a victory that was won 2,000 years ago at Calvary.

Blood and witnesses

Read 1 John 5:6-12

❓ *What might it mean that Jesus came by "water and blood" (v 6)?*
❓ *What testimony is there that this is true?*

❓ *How does John sum up the stark choice we face, and the promise of the gospel?*

In verse 6 John is most likely talking about the baptism and death of Jesus. We've already seen that some people in John's day were saying Jesus wasn't fully God. They said that Christ, the Son of God, came on the human person Jesus at his baptism and left just before he died. They said the man Jesus was filled with the Spirit of Christ during his ministry, but he wasn't really God. By contrast, John says that Jesus was truly and fully God in baptism and in his death. And what John literally says is that Jesus was the Son "through" water and blood—before, during and after his baptism and death. And so with the Holy Spirit, two establish the truth that Jesus is God.

But there's more. These first three witnesses are all the testimony of God towards Christ. But we believe because of the testimony of men (1:1-3; 4:6): the apostolic witness. For us, that means trusting that the Bible gives us an accurate account of that testimony about Jesus: that it is reliable history.

⌄ Apply

This is what we have to share with the world: a story from a book about a man who claimed to be God—with excellent and compelling reasons to be taken seriously.

❓ *Are you able to articulate them to a sceptic? How could you get better?*

Shepherd

As we read Psalm 23, we need to think of David, and then Jesus, singing this psalm, before we learn how to pray it ourselves.

❓ *What do you think are the main ways that a shepherd takes care of sheep?*

Read Psalm 23:1-6

❓ *What does the shepherd in Psalm 23 do for his sheep?*

David, Jesus, us

David: King David sings of how the covenant God brings him, the representative head of Israel, to the place of plentiful provision (v 1-3). This is not the song of any isolated individual. What God does for him, God does (implicitly) for the whole people of God of whom the king is the leader.

Jesus: When the Lord Jesus sang verses 1-3, he would have sung it as the anointed King, the Messiah, the head of the people of God. In this capacity he was confident that God his Father would bring him, and with him all his people, into the place of plenty—the inheritance that is the new heavens and new earth.

Us: What God does for his chosen king, he does for the people of the king. So, as we also are the people of the King—men and women "in Christ"—this blessing and comfort is ours too.

❓ *What impact does this have on your own confidence that God will lead you, guide you and provide for you?*

❓ *Although the shepherd leads his king to "green pastures" (v 1), where else does this path go (v 4)?*

In the dark valley

Verse 4 makes clear that the pathway to these "green pastures" is the road of suffering, as it was in Psalm 22. It takes the king through the "darkest valley". Yet even here, as the king goes into this valley (and as our King Jesus went deep into this valley on the cross), he need ultimately "fear no evil".

✔ Apply

As we follow our King, we too are called to enter the shadow of death, in small ways, through trials and sickness, and in deeper ways, as we face death itself.

❓ *What difference does it make to know that our shepherd walks with us through the valley?*

Our shepherd doesn't walk with us just as individuals but with our church family.

❓ *Who will you encourage with this truth today?*

The King who inherits these covenant assurances is ultimately Jesus Christ. He is the singer of Psalm 23. What comfort this psalm must have brought to him in his earthly sufferings! And now it is ours, as we are "in Christ". Our King has become, with God the Father, our good shepherd, leading us, his sheep, where he has gone before.

How to be sure

John has written this letter because he wants his readers to be sure they're Christians. Throughout the letter he's given them—and us—a number of ways to tell that.

Are you sure?

Read 1 John 5:13

- ❷ *Do you believe in Jesus (see v 1)?*
- ❷ *Do you love other Christians (3:14)?*
- ❷ *Do you continue in your struggle to obey God's commands (2:3)?*
- ❷ *Do you know the testimony of the Spirit (3:24; 4:13)?*

These signs are not a checklist. They merge into one another. But together they show whether we're children of God and whether the gospel has begun to transform our lives.

✔ Apply

- ❷ *Review these signs. How do you match up? If you're not sure, make it your top priority to talk with an older or more mature Christian about these things.*

Confident prayers

Read 1 John 5:14-17

- ❷ *How can we be confident in approaching God in prayer?*
- ❷ *Why is it important to know that God will hear our prayers (v 14), do you think?*
- ❷ *What example does John give of praying in confidence?*
- ❷ *What is "the sin that leads to death" (v 16), do you think?*

If you're a child of God, you can talk to your Father. It's as simple as that. A good father will always take the time to listen to his children; and our Father is always there to listen to his children.

Does prayer change things? We instinctively want to say yes. But does that mean we make God change his mind? The relationship between our prayers and God's will is a mystery. Praying according to God's will can sound a bit like "God answers us when he was going to do it anyway". But we have to remember that our prayers are also part of God's will. God works in us as we pray, just as he works to answer our prayers.

But not all of God's will is mysterious. In the Bible, God has revealed all we need to know of it. And this is John's main concern here. We do know God's will. And so we should pray in the light of God's word. We should remind him of his promises. We should ask for what we know pleases him.

The sin that leads to death is most likely to be rejecting Jesus—turning away from him. God's will is that believers should be continually repenting of sin and finding life in Jesus. God's will is that believers should be holy. That is what we should pray for.

⌃ Pray

Use this understanding to pray for yourself, your friends and family, and your church family.

What you can know

John ends his letter with three great affirmations of faith: "We know... we know... we know..." Confidence in salvation leads to confident prayer and confidence in the truth.

He will keep us
Read 1 John 5:18

- ❓ *Who will keep us safe?*
- ❓ *Who cannot harm a genuine believer?*

It's one thing to have assurance of salvation now, but will it last? What about tomorrow? What about when I face death? John says we can be sure that God will keep us. Satan cannot touch us; he cannot wrestle us out of God's grip. Neither can our sin, because the power of sin in our lives has been decisively broken.

We belong to God
Read 1 John 5:19

- ❓ *How do the two halves of this verse fit together?*
- ❓ *What happens when we forget that the world is under the control of the evil one?*

It can be tough being a Christian. Sometimes it seems that the rest of the world thinks we're crazy. But being sure of our salvation means that we *know* we belong to God. The rest of the world may think we're mad, not because we are but because they are in the grip of Satan's lies. When we forget the truth about the world or the truth about what Jesus has done, we are in danger of falling in love with the world or feeling hopelessly overwhelmed by the opposition.

We know the truth
Read 1 John 5:20

- ❓ *What things do we "know"?*
- ❓ *Why is it not arrogant to be confident about the gospel truths about Jesus?*
- ❓ *Why is it unpopular to be confident about these things today?*

And finally...
Read 1 John 5:21

- ❓ *Why do you think John ends his letter in such a strange way?*
- ❓ *What do you think the idols are that he is referring to?*

Idolatry is making your priority something other than God. Idolatry is settling for a god, or a view of God, that is less than the true God, who can only be found in Christ. Letting the views of the world shape your view of God is idolatry. But Christians have been freed from the lies of Satan. We know the truth. Our confidence in salvation leads to confidence in the truth. For John, this isn't just about reassurance. It's also a challenge not to compromise the truth.

◣ Pray

Have you got what John is driving at repeatedly in this letter? Pray that you would grasp it firmly—and never let go.

2 JOHN: Truth and love

Two tiny letters give us a window into the long-term struggle we face as Christians. How do we sustain the gospel life of our fellowship and message for the long term?

Letter to a dear lady

It's likely that the "lady" being written to is a particular local church, and that her "children" are the Christians who make up the church. The anonymity of the letter may be a reflection of the fact that they were a persecuted minority, and that this was a way of keeping the identity of the recipients secret.

Read 2 John 1-6

- ❓ *What privileges does the "lady" enjoy?*
- ❓ *What is John confident about (v 2-3)?*
- ❓ *What has never changed, according to John?*
- ❓ *Why do you think it's important for the "lady" to know this?*

This elect (chosen) lady can be confident that she enjoys the grace, mercy and truth of God because she has received Jesus. Note the confidence here. These things "will be with" those who have embraced Jesus Christ. Christians can also be completely confident that all true Christians accept and love them. These are facts, not things to aspire to or earn.

Note that truth and love *always* belong together, and that the truth lives in us and will be with us for ever. John is concerned that the dear lady understands this because, if she loses her grip on either, she will lose her confidence in both. And both are under assault by false teachers.

Beware deceivers!

Read 2 John 7-13

- ❓ *What do the deceivers deny?*
- ❓ *What will happen if we listen to them?*
- ❓ *Why is it important to "continue" in the commands?*
- ❓ *Why do you think false teachers remain so prevalent, and why do many find their teaching so compelling?*

False teaching does not often look obvious. False teachers will often dial down the volume of the parts of the gospel we find difficult, or else they offer a strength and confidence in areas where we feel weak and helpless. But their appeal is a sweet-smelling trap that will enslave us and ruin our faith. False teaching drags us from God.

☑ Apply

- ❓ *What do we need to keep confident in?*
- ❓ *How should we respond to deceivers?*
- ❓ *How should we warn others?*

John wants us to know that the stakes are extremely high: life or death, truth or lies, Christ and antichrist. When we lose our grip on Jesus, the only Son of the Father, who came in the flesh, we lose our grip on reality and eternity. We should not welcome false teachers, however positive they seem or widely accepted they are, full stop: not their books, their TV broadcasts or their podcasts.

3 JOHN: First and last

The church has been rocked by many scandals involving those who seek power, prestige and status over loving, humble, open-hearted service. It was always so.

Staying healthy
Read 3 John 1-8

> ❷ *What does John pray for Gaius?*
> ❷ *What brings John the greatest joy?*
> ❷ *What does he encourage Gaius to do?*

Physical health is important, but spiritual health is of far greater significance. Group prayer times can often become an "organ recital", where we pray for an endless list of people's ailments. But John is brought greatest joy when he hears that Gaius is spiritually healthy. Likewise, John told the dear lady in 2 John not to welcome those who twist the truth. Here in 3 John, we are encouraged to welcome, support and encourage those who are fellow workers for the gospel. (In the ancient world, many gospel workers were itinerant preachers.)

☑ Apply

> ❷ *How should the priority of spiritual health shape your prayers together?*
> ❷ *How do you support gospel work? Do you need to change the way you give hospitality, finances and encouragement to those who are fellow gospel workers?*

Healthy leaders
Read 3 John 9-14

> ❷ *What behaviour and attitudes does Diotrephes show that mark him out as a bad thing?*

> ❷ *By contrast, what qualities does Demetrius show that confirm he is the genuine article?*

There is no suggestion in these verses that Diotrephes is a false teacher. Instead the problem is that of a powerful personality who wants to be first. He refuses to accept the authority of John (v 9) or to welcome the itinerant teachers (v 10). He undermines the position of others and expels perceived rivals (v 10) so that he can be first. He may not have a problem with truth, but he has a problem with power. The result is almost as destructive as false teaching.

By contrast, the goodness of Demetrius' character is acknowledged by everyone. "Even by the truth itself" (v 12) means that he taught what was true and his life matched his message. This is the sort of person we must imitate (v 11).

☑ Apply

Someone may be "a great teacher", have bags of personality, be a decisive and strong visionary, and command a lot of respect. And yet, if they have a bullying or dominating personality, it will be toxic to the health of the church.

> ❷ *Can you think of people or situations where this has happened?*
> ❷ *Whose example are you following?*
> ❷ *What will you pray for as a result?*

SONG OF SONGS: Love

What's your favourite love song? What makes it so special? The lyrics? The tune? Or perhaps because you associate it with the one you love?

Read Song of Songs 1:1-4

❷ *Who is speaking?*
❷ *What requests do they make?*

The poem opens with "Let him kiss me" (v 2). It's a call to love. This song celebrates the joy of love and sex within marriage, along with recounting the heartache of unfulfilled longing. But there's more to it than this...

This poem also speaks of God's love for his people and the intimacy he seeks with believers. This is true because God designed marriage to be a picture of Christ's love for the church. But there are other reasons to think that this link is intended by the writer.

1. The woman is likened to the land of Israel, often in ways that don't seem to work as descriptions of human beauty. Is she like Israel or is Israel like a bride? The poem works on both levels. In Isaiah 62:4, God promises, "Your land will be married".

2. The poem is full of garden imagery that takes us back to the Garden of Eden. The poem describes the restoration of the intimacy of Eden that was lost when humanity rebelled against God.

3. The woman is likened to a vineyard, just as God likens Israel to a vineyard (Isaiah 5:1-7).

The greatest love

This poem claims to be the "Song of Songs" (Song of Songs 1:1). It's a way of saying it's the greatest song (just as the "Holy of holies" in the temple was the most holy place). That's a bold claim. Is it really better than all of Solomon's thousand other songs (1 Kings 4:32)?

Yes—this is the greatest song because it celebrates the greatest *love*: the love of Christ for the church. Seeing his love in his word is like receiving a kiss from his mouth (Song of Songs 1:2).

As we walk through this wonderful poem, we'll keep the human lovers we meet there in mind; but it's the love between Christ and his church that will be our focus in these studies.

⌄ Apply

❷ *What signs of Christ's love ("his kisses") have you experienced recently?*
❷ *Why is his love "delightful" (v 2) to you today?*
❷ *In what way is his name "pleasing" (v 3) to you today?*

⌃ Pray

Turn verses 2-4 into an expression of your longing for Jesus.

How beautiful are you?

Without us realising it, our perceptions of beauty are partly linked to wealth and status.

For instance, white Western people often want a tan because in the West darker skin suggests the leisure to go sunbathing.

In Solomon's day, dark skin was unattractive because it signified a peasant who worked in the sun. the woman singer is what we might call today a "redneck" (v 5-6).

Do not stare at me
Read Song of Songs 1:5-6

❷ *How does this woman regard herself?*

In verse 6 she feels the critical stares of the fashionable city girls—just as today we imagine people rating our social-media posts. She's had to neglect her figurative vineyard (her attractiveness) to work in her family's literal vineyards (v 6). Like so many people today, she feels insecure about her appearance.

How beautiful you are
Read Song of Songs 1:7-17

Although she pictures her beloved as her "king" (v 4, 12), he's actually a young shepherd—so she looks for him among the flocks (v 7-8). There the young lovers spend time together on a bed of green foliage with branches forming a roof over their heads (v 16-17). Whenever we spend time listening to Christ's voice in his word and responding in prayer we're spending time enjoying the love of our Beloved (see also v 4).

❷ *How does the man she loves regard her in these verses?*

Verse 9 may not be the best chat-up line to use today! (The jewellery listed in verses 10-11 suggests that verse 9 is a reference to her adornments rather than her physical features.) But his feelings for her are clear in verse 15: "How beautiful you are, my darling!"

Read Ephesians 5:25-27

❷ *What has Christ done for his bride, the church?*
❷ *What is he doing for his bride?*
❷ *What will be the result of his work?*

✔ Apply

❷ *How do you regard yourself?*
❷ *What makes you feel insecure about your identity?*

Perhaps you feel the scrutiny of other people. You imagine them judging your appearance or your performance at work or your commitment to the church. What about the scrutiny of God? Nothing can be hidden from him and his standard is perfection (Hebrews 4:13).

And yet this is what Jesus says to you: "How beautiful you are, my darling!" He looks beyond our sin to see his bride. He sees the beauty he is creating in you.

❷ *What do you want to say to him?*

Bible in a year: 2 Kings 4-6 • Matthew 12 v 24-50 ✔

The rock of refuge

What will it take for you to trust the God and Father of Jesus at all times and even in the face of death? Today's study will be a little different as we meditate on Psalm 31.

Jesus' faith

Read Psalm 31:1-8

Meditate on the trust that Jesus himself showed in his God and Father.

Feel the force of the words "Into your hands I commit my spirit" (v 5).

Read Psalm 31:9-22

Meditate on these verses until you feel the agony of the Lord's sufferings.

Ask God to help you grasp something of the wonder of a man who was under the pressures of verses 9-13 saying, "My times are in your hands" (v 15).

Read Psalm 31:23-24

❓ *When you have meditated afresh on the faith that Jesus showed in his Father, hear again his exhortation to us, his people. How will you respond?*

Your faith

Re-read Psalm 31:6

❓ *What "idols" do you or those you know cling to?*
❓ *What would it look like for you to put your trust wholly in God instead—today?*

Re-read the whole of Psalm 31

As you read it through, make the trust of Jesus your own trust as you enter into his words and heart.

Re-read Psalm 31:15

You may like to make the words "My times are in your hands" very specific, and say not just "my times" in general but "this time" in particular: "This day—this day of pressure, this day of anxiety, this day of persecution, this day of bereavement, even this day of my death—is in your hands".

⌃ Pray

Ask the Lord to help you to use this psalm for the purposes for which God inspired King David to pray it, and King Jesus to fulfil it—that we may walk in Jesus' footsteps, "love the LORD" (v 23) and "be strong and take heart" (v 24) as we "hope" in the God and Father of Jesus, who is the faithful God of unfailing love.

Be ready to pray this again and again, for the pressures of following Jesus will not relent, and you will find your trust wavering.

Don't settle for less

Imagine you find a magic lamp. You give it a rub and a genie appears, offering you one wish. What would you wish for?

Today, the Song invites us not to settle for anything less than true love.

You're the one for me
Read Song of Songs 2:1-3

"I am a rose of Sharon" (v 1) is not a boast. Our female singer is saying that she's a common flower, like any of the many flowers in the valleys. In my locality it would be like saying, "I'm just another buttercup in a field of buttercups. There are thousands of beautiful women in the world, so what makes me so special?" But she is special to her beloved: "a lily among thorns" (v 2). There may be thousands of beautiful women, but there's only one woman for him.

And she feels the same way about him. There may be thousands of other men ("trees of the forest" (v 3), but she only wants to live under his care ("sit in his shade") and enjoy his love ("his fruit is sweet to my taste").

✔ Apply
❷ *Is Jesus the only one for you? Do you look to other "trees" for protection?*
❷ *Does other "fruit" seem sweeter than Jesus? What, and why?*

Yes, but not yet
Read Song of Songs 2:4-7

These verses are an expression of desire ("Let him..."). She looks forward with longing to their wedding day (v 4-5) and wedding night (v 6). But she warns that these passions must not be awakened until the right time (v 7; see also 3:5; 8:4). Perhaps she is asking the city girls not to exert any unhelpful peer pressure.

✔ Apply
❷ *Whatever your current "relationship status", how are you doing all you can to avoid arousing love with the wrong person or at the wrong time, so that sexual love is kept within marriage?*
❷ *In what ways are you most strongly tempted to do the opposite?*

Don't fool about

We were created with desires by God, to lead us to true fulfilment in Christ. But we too easily get diverted en route and settle for lesser joys. So 2:7 is a reminder not to settle for anything less than joy in Christ. As C.S. Lewis famously said, "We are half-hearted creatures, fooling about with drink and sex and ambition when infinite joy is offered to us. We are like an ignorant child who wants to go on making mud pies in the slum because he cannot imagine what is meant by the offer of a holiday at the sea. We are too easily pleased."

Pray for a heart that is satisfied only by Jesus, so that it can be satisfied completely by Jesus.

Come to Christ

You clearly attach some importance to reading the Bible and praying day by day, since here you are reading these notes. But how important is this moment to Christ?

Christ comes to you

Read Song of Songs 2:8-9, 17

The beloved comes to the woman, bounding like a gazelle because he is energised by his love. Picture Christ bounding towards you, energised by love, whenever he sees you opening your Bible.

Come to Christ

Read Song of Songs 2:10-14

Winter has passed and the world is coming into bloom with the arrival of spring. The implication is that now is the time for love to blossom. The longing will soon be over. The cold nights spent waiting will be replaced by the warmth of love. Twice we hear, "Come with me" (v 10, 13).

Apply

In the busyness of our lives and the noise of a godless world, Jesus comes to us with these words: "Arise, come, my darling; my beautiful one, come with me ... Show me your face, let me hear your voice" (v 10, 14). It's an invitation to spend time with him, hearing his love in the words of Scripture and responding with love in the words of our prayers. It's an invitation to his bride, the church, to hear him as we gather each Sunday. It's an invitation to step out of the cold and feel the warmth of his love.

Beware of the foxes

Read Song of Songs 2:15

"The little foxes" might sound cute, but they "ruin the vineyards". Perhaps rats would be a more redolent image today. Remember, too, that in the Song the "vineyard" is an image of sexuality, a place of intimacy (8:12). This verse calls on the wider community to protect young women from "love rats" who would use and abuse them. For Christians, in our relationship with Jesus the foxes represent anything that threatens our enjoyment of Christ by drawing us away from our true love.

Apply

❓ *What stops you coming to Christ each day?*

❓ *What distracts you when you spend time enjoying Christ in prayer?*

Ask God to protect you from these distractions.

He is mine

Read Song of Songs 2:16

Mediate on what it means to say, "Christ belongs to me". Then think deeply about what it means to say, "I belong to Christ".

Now turn your thoughts into prayers to him.

Pursue the one you love

What do we do when Christ seems distant?

It's easy to do nothing when we feel spiritually dry. But that only makes matters worse. These verses show us a better way.

Read Song of Songs 3:1-3

"All night long on my bed" (v 1) suggests that these verses may be a kind of dream sequence. Or they may be a flashback to a stylised version of their courtship and betrothal.

I looked for him

Re-read Song of Songs 3:1-3

❓ *Pick out all the actions the woman takes in these verses.*

She's not passive. She takes the initiative to find her beloved. But instead of finding him, she's found by the watchmen. So she gets them involved in the search (v 3).

⌄ Apply

A time when Christ seems distant is not a time to be passive. We need some "get up and go" (v 2). We need to look for him: in his word as we read it day by day, and among his people as we join with them week by week. We may also need to ask for help.

❓ *Is there something you need to do to pursue Christ?*
❓ *Is there someone you could ask to help you?*

I held him

Read Song of Songs 3:4

❓ *What does the woman do when she finds her beloved?*

She may be bringing him home in order to arrange their wedding. This time, she's going to hold on to him and not let him go.

There's a promise for us in these verses: "I looked for the one my heart loves ... I found the one my heart loves" (v 1, 4). Times of spiritual dryness are part of most Christian lives—we don't live on a constant emotional high. But Christ is not hiding from us. "Seek and you will find," he assures us (Matthew 7:7).

Read Song of Songs 3:5

Perhaps this renewed exhortation is prompted by what the watchmen have been saying, which may have been something like, *Why look for an absent lover when are there other suitable bachelors at hand?* "There are plenty more fish in the sea," we might say today. But there's only one man to whom she will give her love, and she will not give herself to him until they are bound together in the covenant of marriage.

⌃ Pray

Lord, may I have eyes only for you, so that all the other things I love are part of my love for you rather than rivals to my love for you. Amen.

Wedding bells

At the beginning of a wedding the bride makes her big entrance. That's what we see here.

Who's her king?

Read Song of Songs 3:6-10

❓ *How does the bride describe her beloved?*

I think the beloved is almost certainly not Solomon, not least because the Song ends by comparing the way the woman has protected "her vineyard" (her sexuality) to the way Solomon rented his out (by having numerous wives and concubines—1 Kings 11:1-3). The link between Solomon and the Song in Song of Songs 1:1 need not mean the Song is about him or by him. It could have been commissioned by Solomon or associated with the golden age of wisdom over which he presided.

So who is this? It's her shepherd-lover, whom she's already described as her "king" (1:4, 12).

❓ *If this is not actually Solomon, what effect does the bride achieve by describing her wedding, and her husband-to-be, in this way?*

Perhaps she's still dreaming, and in her dreams she imagines a fairy-tale wedding in which she marries her prince (3:1). Or perhaps this is an exaggerated description of their marriage, highlighting the way she considers him to be the greatest of men. He sends a noble bodyguard and luxurious carriage so she can travel to her wedding in safety and comfort.

Our Shepherd-King

Perhaps it's no accident that the beloved is a king-like shepherd. It reminds us of the Lord whom David describes as "my shepherd" (Psalm 23:1). It reminds us of David himself, the shepherd boy who became Israel's greatest king (2 Samuel 5:1-2). And it points forward to David's greater son, Jesus. Jesus is the King who came to be the good Shepherd, who laid down his life for his sheep (John 10:11).

The column of smoke in Song of Songs 3:6 is perfumed with "incense"—it's literally "frankincense". Yet incense couldn't be used as personal perfume because it only releases its scent when burnt. It was, however, used in the tabernacle. Indeed, that was the only place where it was to be used (Exodus 30:34-38). In the tabernacle, burning incense reminded the people of God's coming to his people in the clouds of Mount Sinai and leading them by means of the pillar of cloud. Now in Song of Songs 3:6, a pillar of cloud is coming through the wilderness to lead a bride to her wedding. This marriage is a picture of God redeeming his people, making a covenant with us and leading us home.

⌄ Apply

❓ *How does all this imagery excite you about being loved by, and in love with, King Jesus?*

You've stolen my heart

Chapter 3 described the wedding of the two lovers. In chapter 4, we see them on their wedding night.

Read Song of Songs 4:1-11

How beautiful you are

If you didn't read these verses aloud, then do so now (though you might want to be careful who overhears you!).

- ❓ *How does the beloved praise his wife's beauty (v 1-7)?*
- ❓ *How does he feel about her love for him (v 8-10)?*
- ❓ *How does he describe her kisses (v 11)?*

The language is tender yet powerful. It's erotic and sensual without ever being smutty. It includes language we've heard before (compare 4:1 and 1:15, and 4:10 and 1:2-3). But now this is taken to another level because the couple have arrived at the wedding night. The restraint they have previously shown (2:7; 3:5) is no longer needed. Her hair is no longer up as then befitted a modest woman in public; now for him it tumbles down like a flock of goats cascading down a hillside (4:1). Verse 8 perhaps reflects her nervousness, so he invites her to leave her fears and descend into his embrace.

Here is a man delighting in his new bride. "You have stolen my heart, my sister, my bride" (v 9). We can only imagine what it felt like to hear these words.

✔ Apply

If you're married, review how you speak to your spouse.

- ❓ *Do you praise his or her beauty and express your delight in their love?*
- ❓ *How could you do so more, or more tenderly? (And not just their physical beauty but their spiritual beauty too.)*

Sheep, towers... honey

It's easy to mock this husband's comparison of his wife's teeth to sheep or of her neck to a tower. Every culture has its own distinctive language for love. Future generations may find it strange that we name our loved ones after the viscous secretion of insects (i.e. honey). But perhaps our mockery is also a sign that we're missing the point. What is being described is a landscape. This is God describing his people, represented by their land.

Re-read Song of Songs 4:8-11, but this time read it as Christ's words to you. As you do so, leave your fears behind and descend into his embrace.

▲ Pray

And now speak to Jesus in response to his words to you.

Consummated love

In these verses we reach the climax of the story and the song.

Him to her

Read Song of Songs 4:12-15

Throughout the Song, the bride's sexuality is likened to a vineyard or garden. Until now, it has been "a garden locked up" and "a sealed fountain" (v 12). In other words, she is a virgin who has not given herself away.

The description in chapter 4 has moved down the woman's body. In verses 14-15 it moves further down and becomes still more intimate. But there is nothing crude in her husband's description of her. Instead, the language becomes even more figurative, as if to hide her modesty. She is an orchard of fruits and spices, creating a profusion of scents that delight his senses (v 14).

Her to him

Read Song of Songs 4:16

For the first time on their wedding night, the bride speaks. She picks up his garden imagery and calls on the winds to waft her scents to entice her lover. "You are a garden", he said in verse 12; now she describes her sexuality as "his garden" and invites him to enter. "Do not awaken..." she said before their wedding (2:7; 3:5). But now she cries out, "Awake": "Let my beloved come into his garden and taste its choice fruits".

Time to leave

The time has come for us quietly to leave the lovers to their love-making. In 5:1 we switch from the present tense to the present perfect tense—we only return to their story after their love-making is complete.

Read Song of Songs 5:1

4:16 – 5:1 is the exact middle point of this song. The woman's invitation to love and the consummation of that love form both the poetic and sexual climax of their story.

☑ Apply

In Eden, humanity enjoyed an intimate relationship with God. Now, through the Song, we are again invited to re-enter the garden and enjoy Jesus, our Bridegroom. Not all of us are married; and of those that are, some of us are not happily married, and some of us are part of happy marriages that, for one reason or another, find sex difficult or impossible. So not all of us enjoy the sexual intimacy described in these verses. But the invitation to spiritual intimacy is extended to *everyone*. And this is not a second-best option because intimacy with Christ is the ultimate love to which human marriage and sex points. The application of these verses is for all of us to hear these words from Jesus: "Eat, friends, and drink; drink your fill of love" (5:1).

> ❷ *How will you pray in response to this invitation?*

My help and deliverer

In Psalm 40, David sings about himself and what happens between him and the covenant God. But what happens to the king shapes what will happen to his people.

He turned to me

Read Psalm 40:1-10

- ❓ *What does God do for the king (v 1-3)?*
- ❓ *In verse 3, David is given a "new song". What do you think he might have sung about God?*
- ❓ *What did David tell the people (v 9-10)?*

The king comes to the front of his choir and sings, "I waited patiently for the LORD" (v 1). God heard that prayer. From "the slimy pit … mud and mire"—that poetic image of weakness and impending death—God has lifted him up, set his feet "on a rock" (a place of solidity) and given him "a new song", in which he praises God for rescuing him. We come in at the end of verse 3: "Many will see"—that is, see God rescue his chosen king—"and fear the LORD". They too—and we too—will "put their trust in him".

- ❓ *When the old-covenant people saw God rescue their king, how would that have helped them to put their own trust in God?*
- ❓ *When we see how God the Father raised Jesus his Son, our King, from the "slimy pit" of death, how does that encourage us to put our trust in God?*

Our hope depends entirely on the resurrection and ascension of Jesus. As we join him in singing verses 9-10, our hearts lift with joy, knowing that the God and Father of Jesus is indeed the God of unchanging love and faithfulness, in whom we can safely trust.

✔ Apply

Psalm 40:1-3 can become our story in Christ. We, too, can wait patiently in times of trial, confident that the day will come when, in Christ, we will have a new song in our mouths: a song that celebrates the way God has rescued us from the slimy pit of death.

- ❓ *When might you most need to rest in this truth this week?*

Think of me

Read Psalm 40:11-17

- ❓ *What is the contrast between verses 1-10 and 11-17?*
- ❓ *Does this surprise you? Why / why not?*

It seems most likely that v 11-17 are revisiting the troubles from which David has been rescued—the point seems to be that the king's troubles arise out of his self-offering as the sacrifice for his people's sins (v 6-8).

Re-read Psalm 40:16

Here, the king prays for his people: that they may have joy and gladness and "always say, 'The LORD is great!'" This—for us—is the climax of the psalm: that we, as the King's people, rejoice in the God and Father of Jesus, and celebrate his greatness.

- ❓ *When would saying to yourself, "The LORD is great" make most difference to you this week?*

Bible in a year: 2 Kings 24-25 • Matthew 17 ✔

Longing

"The course of true love never did run smooth," said William Shakespeare. It was ever thus…

In 5:1, we see the consummation of the lovers' love. But we've not arrived at a happy-ever-after moment—not yet.

Read Song of Songs 5:2-8

> ❓ *Can you reconstruct the scene? What do you think is going on here?*
> ❓ *Can you trace this woman's emotions as the mini-drama unfolds?*

Perhaps he's arrived home unexpectedly. Perhaps she's not in the mood tonight. Perhaps it's simply late, and she's already tucked up in bed (v 3). Whatever the scenario, it's clear that his desires are frustrated. When he gets no response, he gives up (v 3-4). In the meantime, though, her desire has been aroused by his desire (v 4-5), but by then it's too late (v 6). When she can't find her beloved, she becomes reckless and "faint with love" (v 7-8).

Placing this episode immediately after the consummation of love in verse 1 is significant. Suddenly we lurch from climax to crisis. It's a reminder that human love is fragile and fleeting. Even the most intense moments of passion are soon over, and even the best marriages have their tensions.

The author and family expert Christopher West says, "God gave us sexual desire … as the fuel of a rocket that is meant to launch us into the stars and beyond". At the heart of human experience is longing—a longing that points us to fulfilment in God. As the fourth-century bishop Augustine famously

said, "Our hearts are restless until they find their rest in you".

> ❓ *How do moments of romantic joy and sexual pleasure point us to God?*
> ❓ *How do frustrated longings and relational heartache point us to God?*

⌄ Apply

Even our experience of divine love can feel fleeting in this life. There are moments of intense joy, but they don't last. Think about your relationship with God.

> ❓ *Look back over recent months or years. Can you trace moments of great joy and times when your spiritual life felt flat?*

Both the highs and lows are meant to point us forward to the day when we see Christ face to face. The question is, when Christ comes knocking, can you be bothered?

> ❓ *How does this passage help you have a realistic and positive understanding of your relationship with Jesus?*
> ❓ *If you are married, how does it help you to navigate the ups and downs of your own relationship?*

⌃ Pray

Lord, may my desires lead me to you, and may my frustrations fuel my longing for your return. Amen.

Altogether lovely

Song of Songs 5:2-8 introduced the theme of unfulfilled longing. Now the friends prompt the woman to remind herself of why she loves her beloved.

Read Song of Songs 5:9-16

> ❓ *What's your favourite line in this rich description?*

The conclusion is clear: "He is altogether lovely" (v 16).

···· **TIME OUT** ··

Read Revelation 1:12-18

> ❓ *What's your favourite line in this rich description?*

His mouth is sweetness

Re-read Song of Songs 5:16

We can't see Christ. But we can hear his voice when we read his word or hear it preached. Paul says, "The light of the gospel … displays the glory of Christ" (2 Corinthians 4:4). We see by hearing. We see the beauty of Christ when we hear the gospel message.

> ❓ *Recall some of the stories of Jesus in the Gospels. What do they reveal about his character?*

The conclusion is clear: Jesus is the "altogether lovely" one (Song of Songs 5:16).

We don't need to allegorise all the details of the description in verses 10-15. The point is that in the bride's eyes the beloved is altogether lovely. In the same way, when we look at Christ, we see one who is altogether lovely.

This is my friend

Re-read Song of Songs 5:16

There's no doubt that the lovers find each other physically attractive. But their love is more than skin-deep. They are also friends.

> ❓ *If you're married, are you cultivating a friendship with your spouse?*
> ❓ *If you're a Christian, are you cultivating a friendship with Christ?*

Read Song of Songs 6:1-3

Verse 2 recalls their sexual union in 5:1. He may be temporarily absent (5:6), but he's not permanently lost to her. What matters is that they're married, and therefore she belongs to him and he to her (6:3).

When Christ feels absent, we can rely on his covenant. He has promised himself to us. That covenant promise is confirmed and reiterated in baptism and the Lord's Supper. In baptism Christ says, *I am yours and you are mine,* and that mutual commitment is reaffirmed whenever we receive bread and wine.

🔼 Pray

> ❓ *Is there some characteristic of Christ that has caught your imagination today?*

If Christ feels distant, remind yourself of how he is altogether lovely. With this in mind, gives thanks that you can say, "I am my beloved's and my beloved is mine".

You complete me

We sometimes talk about "feeling empty"—which raises the question: what truly fills you up?

Read Song of Songs 6:4-10

These verses echo the description of 4:1-3, but without its more erotic dimensions, perhaps because these are the first words of reconciliation after the break in relationship in chapter 5. Renewed sexual intimacy will come in chapter 7, once the relationship is repaired. Nevertheless the husband's desire is evident: her eyes "overwhelm" him (6:5).

Tirzah (v 4) was the original capital of the northern kingdom of Israel (until King Omri built Samaria), while Jerusalem was the capital of the southern kingdom of Judah. Once again, this description pushes us beyond the two young lovers to see God's desire for his people, represented by their capital cities.

King Solomon had 700 wives and 300 concubines (1 Kings 11:3). So Song of Songs 6:8 suggests this poem is set (though not necessarily written) while Solomon was still forming his harem. In contrast to Solomon's promiscuity, the Song affirms that true blessing is found in covenant fidelity to one person. This is true of both human marriage and our relationship to Christ.

Read Song of Songs 6:11-12

These verses are hard to interpret. If the garden is literal, then it seems to be the place where the lovers were reunited and reconciled. If it's figurative, then it's a reminder of sexual bliss. In either case, the husband's desires are fulfilled.

Read Song of Songs 6:13

There's no known place called Shulam. So "Shulammite" probably means "the woman of peace", because the Hebrew word for deep peace or contentment is "shalom". His wife is this man's "shalom-bringing woman", who makes him feel complete and content. Her name is a promise of desire fulfilled.

This is a reminder that God made humanity male and female, to be united in marriage, and that it's therefore "not good for [humans] to be alone" (Genesis 1:27; 2:18). But we also need to remember that human sexuality was created by God to point to Christ's relationship with the church (Ephesians 5:25-27). Written into the sex of our bodies is a reminder that we're ultimately only complete in Christ.

⌄ Apply

- ❓ *What happens when we look to a human being other than Jesus to make us feel complete?*
- ❓ *Are you in any danger of doing this? How, and why?*
- ❓ *If you are married, how can you be a "peace-bringing" spouse?*

⌃ Pray

Is anything making you discontented or envious? Confess this to Christ in prayer and ask him to make you feel complete in him.

How he thinks of you

How do you think Christ views you? Why do you think that?

Perhaps you think he tolerates you. Or that he loves you because to love is the right thing to do, but you can't imagine he feels any affection for you.

Read Song of Songs 6:13

"Let's have a look at her," demand the friends. But the man rejects their attempt to make his wife an object to be assessed or ranked. He will describe her beauty in 7:1-9; but to see it is for his eyes only. His love-making with her is not for public consumption.

☑ Apply

Job said, "I made a covenant with my eyes not to look lustfully at a young woman" (Job 31:1).

❷ *Do you need to follow Job's example?*

His desire is for me

Read Song of Songs 7:1-7

Beginning with the dancing feet of 6:13, the beloved moves up her body, delighting in everything he sees. He is captivated by what he sees. It's as if she's tied up his heart with her hair (7:5).

❷ *How do you think she felt when she heard this description?*

Read Song of Songs 7:8-10

Verses 8-9 are a statement of his intent to consummate their love in sexual union, and

she welcomes his advances. He says her kisses are like wine, so she invites him to drink them in. Rejoicing in his desire, she gives herself to him in love (v 10).

The word "desire" in verse 10 is the word used to describe the curse of marital conflict in Genesis 3:16. In the couple's personal Eden, the curse is turned to blessing, for this is a loving, giving, intimate desire rather than a self-centred, wrestling sinful one.

Once again, we don't need to allegorise all the details of this description. The point is that in this husband's eyes his wife is beautiful, pleasing and full of delights (Song of Songs 7:6). And in Christ's eyes we are beautiful. He takes pleasure in his bride. He takes pleasure in you. He desires to love you and enjoy you in what older writers called "mystical union". His desire recreates the blessing of Eden.

☑ Apply

❷ *Do you hear the intensity of Jesus' desire for you? How will that change your view of yourself, and of your relationship with him?*

❷ *Will you seek to match his longing for you with a longing for him?*

Next time you pray or meet as a church or home group, don't ask yourself whether you got something out of it. Ask yourself, "Did Christ enjoy it? Did it satisfy his desire for his people?"

Come, let us go

"With my body I thee worship," say the old Anglican wedding vows.

Read Song of Songs 7:11-13

Throughout the Song of Songs, the woman's vineyard has been a picture of her sexuality. So verse 12 may be an invitation to see if she is aroused. If she is, then she will give herself to him in love. She will offer him "every delicacy" of love (v 13). This is her response to the desire he expressed in verses 1-9. Verse 12 may also be an invitation to see whether their love-making will result in fruit in the sense of children.

⌄ Apply

What is the proper response of the church to Christ's love?

Read Romans 12:1

- ❓ *What does "proper worship" look like?*
- ❓ *How does God feel about us offering our bodies in this way?*
- ❓ *What is it that motivates us to offer ourselves in this way?*
- ❓ *What will it mean for you to use your body in this way today?*

···· TIME OUT ····

Read Isaiah 5:1-7

- ❓ *Israel, like the woman, is pictured as a vineyard. What does God find when he looks for fruit?*

Read John 15:1-8

- ❓ *How can we bear fruit for God?*

Embraced
Read Song of Songs 8:1-3

Our singer wants to kiss her beloved all the time but obeys the constraints of public decency (v 1). So she leads him to the intimacy of her family home. The longing to be entwined in each other's arms which was expressed in the dream of 2:6 is now a reality.

⌄ Apply

In a lovely aside, we discover that the woman has learnt how to love from observing the example of her mother (8:2). We, too, learn how to how to love Christ from mothers and fathers in the faith (Titus 1:4; 2:3-5).

- ❓ *Is there an older Christian who could mentor you?*
- ❓ *Is there a younger Christian whom you could mentor?*

Reminded
Read Song of Songs 8:4

For a third time we are warned not to arouse love until it finds its true expression in marriage.

- ❓ *Why might a reader (especially an unmarried one) need to hear this again at this point, do you think?*
- ❓ *In what way do you need to hear it?*

Stronger than death

"Money can't buy me love," sang the Beatles. So, what is love worth? And how long does it last?

The flames of passion
Read Song of Songs 8:5-7

Death, the grave and fire are destructive powers; but love is their equal (v 6). Uncontrolled erotic love can wreak a world of harm. But within the constraints of marriage, it is a powerful force for good.

So these verses are both a warning and a promise. They reiterate the warning of verse 4: once awakened, illicit love cannot easily be contained or controlled. But covenant love promises a lifetime of joy "until death us do part".

To the church in our relationship with our Husband, this a promise "that neither death nor life ... will be able to separate us from the love of God that is in Christ Jesus our Lord" (Romans 8:38-39). The love of Christ is not just as strong as death; it is stronger than death, for his love defeated death when he died in our place on the cross and rose again in triumph. Even death cannot part us from him and his love.

Given and not bought
Read Song of Songs 8:7-12

❷ *What is the advice given in verses 8-9?*
❷ *What do verses 7 and 11-12 say about love and sex?*

Young people are to be protected from those who would use and abuse their sexuality (v 8-9). Love given away cheaply loses its value (v 7, 11; see 1 Kings 11:1-6). A woman's sexuality is something for her to give without coercion (Song of Songs 7:12).

In 1:6 the bride-to-be was shy and insecure; now in 8:10 she thrusts out her breasts in confidence. What has made the difference? His love. It is "his eyes" that have changed her view of herself (8:10). She has become his contentment—his shalom-bringing woman (6:13; 8:10).

✅ Apply

❷ *What difference will the Lord Jesus' love for you make to you? What difference will knowing how he sees you make to your confidence today?*

Let me hear your voice
Read Song of Songs 8:13-14

In verses 13-14 the cycle begins again as the lovers renew their love-making, echoing what they have said before (2:9, 13-14). And today Christ comes to you to renew his relationship with you, and says, "Let me hear your voice".

⬆ Pray

Pray that the loving eyes of Christ would relieve your doubts and calm your fears. Thank him that whatever happens in this life and in death, he will love you.

Put your hope in God

Although Psalms 42 and 43 are separate in the original manuscripts, there are good reasons for studying them, and praying them, together.

Read Psalms 42 and 43

❓ *What refrain is repeated three times across these two psalms?*

❓ *What other similarities are there?*

When lonely

Psalm 42 begins with a deer panting desperately for life-giving waters. It is the only way the psalmist can describe his desperate longing for God. In verse 4, he remembers "the house of God"—the Jerusalem Temple—and the people of God gathering for one of the great Old Testament covenant festivals, like Passover ("the festive throng"). What he misses is not some solitary experience of God but the corporate throng of enthusiastic temple worship. When we sing this, we express an intense longing for the immediate presence of God the Father, and for the joy of being in the new heavens and new earth, led by Jesus our worship-leader as we sing songs of exultant praise and joy.

❓ *How does the corporate worship in your church partially satisfy this longing?*

❓ *Does this change how you think about your local church? How?*

When under pressure

❓ *What three watery images do we see in verses 1, 3 and 7?*

The joyful sound of thronging crowds is replaced by the sound of overwhelming waters. This is Bible poetry for chaos and terror. Not only is the psalmist far from the people of God rejoicing in the presence of God; he is under overwhelming pressure. In verses 9 and 10 we learn what is causing the terrifying waters: enemies. It is wonderful to think of Jesus praying verses 6-11, as he faced the terrifying floodwaters of human hostility, the concrete expression of the Father's wrath pouring over him, drowning his soul in sorrows as they swept over him. And yet in the midst of it all, the Father's love was unchanging (v 8a).

❓ *Are you facing pressures and troubles that come with following Jesus? How can this section help you to talk to yourself with words of realistic faith?*

When you're rejected

Re-read Psalm 43

❓ *Verse 1 is the first explicit prayer in these psalms. What does the psalmist pray for, and why?*

❓ *Having reminded himself that God is his "stronghold" (v 2), what does he ask God to do (v 3-4)?*

He holds two things in tension: his disturbed state of mind and his certainty that he will again praise God. So he can say to himself repeatedly, "Put your hope in God".

❓ *Looking ahead to the coming week, when might you need to talk to yourself in this same way?*

2 CORINTHIANS: Messy

When it comes to serving Jesus in the messiness and complexity of the church and our world, the letter of 2 Corinthians is the place to start.

....

Paul both loved the Corinthians and was driven nuts by them in equal measure. He has more recorded interaction with them than with any other church he planted. And at the point he wrote 2 Corinthians, it was still not clear whether the church would flourish and grow or crash and burn—which explains why this is the most passionate, honest, vulnerable, heartfelt letter in the Bible.

In the first chapter, Paul wants to make sure that whatever the Corinthians are going through, they have got the fact that God himself is the foundation of life and ministry.

To the church of God

Read 2 Corinthians 1:1-3

❷ *What names appear most often in these verses?*

❷ *How does Paul see himself? How does he describe his readers?*

Undergirding everything that Paul writes in this letter is the fact that God rules and provides for his church. The church is not our project; it is God's. So Paul isn't pursuing his own agenda but God's.

❷ *How does verse 2 reflect that view?*

❷ *What situations can you think of in which grace and peace would help?*

The deceptively rich phrase in verse 2 opens every letter that Paul wrote to a church. It encapsulates all that God the Father holds out to us in the Lord Jesus Christ through the gospel. Grace and peace are what we all need—and what God gives us. So our life as God's people should be marked by grace and peace, making our churches the most accepting and forgiving communities on the planet. All this starts with God.

The Father of mercies

❷ *In verse 3, what else does Paul say that God provides?*

In the New Testament, the word "comfort" is a long way from the warm fuzziness we tend to think of. It includes everything from an arm round the shoulder to a kick in the pants! In John's Gospel, Jesus describes the Holy Spirit as the "Comforter"—the One who convicts us of sin, strengthens us, emboldens us and transforms us.

🔼 Pray

What situations do you know of in your church that need grace, peace, mercy or comfort? Pray for them now.

Praise God for the way he has provided for you, and blessed you and your church.

Ask God to prepare your heart to study this letter. Pray that he would teach, challenge, encourage and comfort you.

Suffering and comfort

God is the God of all comfort—but this comfort (or encouragement) is not designed to stop with one person.

Read 2 Corinthians 1:3-7

❓ *Who comforts who? Trace the chain of comfort that Paul describes.*

Paul assumes that the Christian life is one of suffering and strengthening, of setbacks and encouragement, of struggle and joy. That's what we can expect. We face difficulties. God encourages us. We encourage others. Repeat.

❓ *How is this reflected in your own experience?*

We need to be prepared for life to be painful, sore and hard. The good news is that pain is the very experience in which we will receive the encouragement of God through Christ—which will enable us to encourage others.

But we can only share what we have received ourselves. If we are to serve Christ, then the comfort of the gospel has to be real and fresh for us. That's why we need to keep reading the Bible, speaking the gospel into one another's lives, and gathering as the church to hear the comforting voice of God.

If...

❓ *What two scenarios does Paul describe in verse 6?*
❓ *What is the result of each one?*
❓ *What does that lead Paul to say in verse 7?*

God will deliver us

Read 2 Corinthians 1:8-11

Paul knows his readers need to be utterly convinced not only that there is purpose in suffering now but that there is hope beyond suffering. So here he shares what God has taught him for the encouragement of others.

❓ *How does Paul describe the situation he was in?*
❓ *How did this affliction actually build Paul's faith?*

Our regular experience of God working in and through our suffering is the testimony that our future is utterly secure in Christ. One day, he will bring us out of suffering to be with himself for ever.

In verse 11, Paul asks the Corinthians to pray for him. In a way, this is a further application of verses 4-5. We pray for each other as we suffer, and as one group of Christians sees God delivering and strengthening another, they are encouraged.

Apply

❓ *Where do you seek comfort when you are suffering?*
❓ *How could you encourage other Christians you know who are suffering?*
❓ *What difference does it make that God will deliver us in the end?*

Keeping promises

Why should I trust you? Why should you trust me?

These questions are at the heart of this passage. Paul said he was coming to Corinth and then didn't show up. This seriously damaged his relationship with the Corinthians. Now Paul is pleading, *TRUST ME!*

Read 2 Corinthians 1:12-22

> ❷ *What reason does Paul give to trust him in verse 12?*

It is because of the transformation that Paul has found in Christ that he can boast about his conscience. He's not saying he is perfect, but by the grace of God his actions have been characterised by transparent sincerity.

In verses 13-14 he underlines this: he hasn't been showing off but seeking to help the Corinthians get the truth about Jesus.

⬆ Pray

Lord, I want to behave with simplicity and godly sincerity, not by earthly wisdom but by your grace. Please help me to rely on you so that I look like you more and more. Please help me to boast in you alone—recognising that when I have a clear conscience, it is because of you. Amen.

Making plans

In verses 15-16 Paul explains that he planned to visit the Corinthians in order to encourage them further.

> ❷ *What did Paul's change of plans seem like (v 17)?*
> ❷ *Why might that have been frustrating to the Corinthians?*
> ❷ *But what has remained consistent (v 18-20)?*

God has shown himself to be utterly dependable in Christ. We are to answer God's faithfulness with our own—uttering our own "Amen" to God for his glory (v 20). We are to be reliable and do what God tells us.

> ❷ *What help are we given in that (v 21-22)?*

Paul and his companions can be depended upon to put the gospel of Christ first. That will mean, at times, being flexible and reordering their priorities to do what is best for the spread of the gospel.

We, too, should be dependably flexible. That doesn't mean being disorganised and unreliable but putting the gospel first and arranging our lives around Christ's priorities.

⬇ Apply

> ❷ *In what areas could you become more reliable or dependable?*
> ❷ *Do you get frustrated with others who seem unreliable? How could this passage help you to be patient with them?*
> ❷ *What plans might you need to change for the sake of the gospel?*

Robust love

So why hadn't Paul come back to visit the Corinthians? It was because he loved them.

Read 2 Corinthians 1:23 – 2:4

- ❓ *What does Paul say he wants for the Corinthians (v 24; 2:4)?*
- ❓ *What actions has that led him to take (1:23; 2:1, 4)?*

Paul knew that if he showed up again, he would have to confront and correct them again, at a time when they were still raw from his last visit. This would have made them all miserable (v 1).

But Paul felt the pain of being robbed of the joy of seeing them flourish (v 2-3). So, instead, working for their lasting joy, he wrote a tear-stained, love-saturated letter (v 4)—which is not in the New Testament.

This is the strong love that God has shown us, and the strong love that God has called us to: love that weeps instead of raging when others get things wrong.

For your sake

Read 2 Corinthians 2:5-11

- ❓ *Why else did Paul write his previous letter (v 9)?*
- ❓ *What instruction has he just told them to obey, and why (v 6-8)?*

Paul's discipline of the Corinthians is not vindictive. Previously, he had encouraged them to deal firmly with someone who had sinned spectacularly and publicly (probably the events alluded to in 1 Corinthians

5:1-5). They have done this. But now, in 2 Corinthians 2:5-8, he tells them that enough is enough: it is time to forgive.

There is a danger of playing right into Satan's hands, both by ignoring church discipline on the one hand and by becoming harsh and condemning on the other (v 11). Sin and repentance must both be taken seriously for the sake of the Corinthians and the gospel (v 10).

- ❓ *How does Paul exemplify this in the way he deals with the Corinthians?*

✓ Apply

Think how striking it would be in our world if we dealt well with both sin and repentance, taking sin seriously and then showing forgiveness and restoration. That would be truly robust love. Godly love. Love which can be trusted.

- ❓ *When have you seen Christians be too harsh and condemning? What was the result?*
- ❓ *When have you seen Christians be too soft and forgiving? What was the result?*
- ❓ *How does the combination of dealing seriously with sin and being quick to restore reflect the way God treats us in Christ?*
- ❓ *How can we remind ourselves of what God's robust love is like, to help ourselves love one another well?*

A powerful smell

We know Paul's top priority was to proclaim the gospel. But what did that actually look like? And can we ever be like him?

Read 2 Corinthians 2:12-13

❓ *Why did Paul change his plans, and what does that tell us about his priorities?*

Paul isn't just a truth-proclaiming machine. Christ-like ministry means he really cares for the people he works with and serves.

⌄ Apply

Paul's attitude raises the question: what kind of brother or sister in Christ are you going to be? Will you just put your head down and run your own life and ministry your own way? Or will you serve with head up and heart open—noticing and acting when your fellow Christians need encouragement?

❓ *Does anything need to change? How?*

Fragrance
Read 2 Corinthians 2:14-17

Paul paints a picture of a victory parade in Rome. What does it mean that God "leads us" in such a procession (v 14)? The NIV says we are led "as captives". But really Paul means we are the incense-bearers. We follow Christ, our victorious general, carrying incense, which produces fragrant smoke.

❓ *What is the fragrance, and who spreads it (v 14)?*

In verse 15 Paul shifts the image to say we are actually the smell itself.

❓ *What is the source of this aroma?*
❓ *What difference does it make that it rises "to" God but "among" people?*

Both those who have opposed the gospel and those who have been rescued by it breathe in the incense (v 15-16).

❓ *In a victory parade, why would the smell evoke death for some and life for others?*
❓ *Why does the gospel message bring both those reminders?*

"Who is equal to such a task?" asks Paul (v 16). Who is up to the task of proclaiming the gospel and its message of life and death? Surprisingly, the answer isn't *Nobody* but *We are*! Why? Because of the power of the gospel.

❓ *In verse 17, how does Paul describe what it means to preach the gospel?*

Incense-bearers don't have to create the aroma—they just show up and hold the incense, and the smoke does the rest. This is the role that God gives to us. Are we up to the task of gospel ministry? Yes, if we are prepared to speak in the power of Christ about Christ with sincerity—because it is God who speaks through us.

⌃ Pray

Ask for God's help in proclaiming the truth of Christ in the power of Christ this week.

Bible in a year: Jeremiah 20-21 • Matthew 24 v 1-28 ✓

Sufficient

The question which Paul raised in 2:16 is still on his mind: how do we know we are up to the task of proclaiming the gospel?

❓ *How and why might you be tempted to prove you are a good Christian?*

❓ *What reasons might you have for being underconfident in ministry or in your walk with God?*

This passage is very clear: we aren't sufficient in ourselves, but our sufficiency is from God. God not only speaks but changes people through the gospel. That means that, despite all our inadequacy, we can keep going and get on with the job.

Read 2 Corinthians 3:1-4

Paul really is commending himself in these verses. But it's not because he has a great résumé.

❓ *What does Paul say are the only credentials he needs (v 2)?*

❓ *Who wrote this "letter" of recommendation (v 3)?*

What God has done in the Corinthians through his preaching far outstrips even the definitive moment in the history of the nation of Israel when Moses received the law on "tablets of stone" on Mount Sinai (see Exodus 32:15-16).

From glory to glory

Read 2 Corinthians 3:4-11

❓ *Why can we have confidence in ministry?*

Verse 6 unlocks everything that Paul says here. Our adequacy comes from the fact that God has equipped and appointed us as "ministers of a new covenant": a covenant under which God actually changes people.

❓ *What was good about the covenant God made with Moses (v 7)?*

❓ *What is even better about the new covenant and the ministry of the Spirit?*

Moses' ministry was remarkable—his face was literally radiant because he had been in the presence of God (see Exodus 34:29-35)—but that ministry couldn't itself actually bring about deep change in anyone, nor were the effects it had on Moses himself permanent. But new-covenant ministry brings actual righteousness: real change.

☑ Apply

❓ *What makes you hesitate to have confidence that God can really change people?*

❓ *How does today's passage help?*

❓ *Who could you invest in, as Paul invested in the Corinthians, to be able to say they are your "letter of recommendation"?*

❓ *Whose "letter of recommendation" are you? Who could you encourage by sharing how God has been working in your life?*

Success and shame

This psalm expresses the normal Christian experience: both our trust in God for our final victory and the suffering and shame that come along the way.

Read Psalm 44:1-8

- ❓ *As the psalmist looks back, what does he remember about God?*
- ❓ *What do you think it means to "make our boast" in God "all day long" (v 8)?*

Verses 1-3 look back to reaffirm that the promised land was a gift from God. It was God who "drove out the nations" and "planted" his people in the land (v 2). In verse 4 an individual comes to the front of the choir and claims a covenant relationship with God. He speaks and sings as a leader of the people of God. And so we begin to hear the voice of the great leader of the people of God as he leads his choir. But verse 9 comes as a shock. The music changes sharply...

Read Psalm 44:9-26

- ❓ *Can you spot these themes in verses 9-26? Expect defeat; anticipate shame; pledge loyalty; pray urgently.*

An absent God, a defeated army, a plundered people, a devoured people, a scattered people. What a sorry sight. And these are the people led by the leader who trusts God for victory! And yet in some way this is the typical experience of the people of God; it's to be expected, for the pattern of Bible expectation shapes the church of God not to be surprised when those who follow God's leader experience suffering.

- ❓ *How does Romans 8:17 express this same truth?*

Both "I" and "we"

First, let us focus on the individual who comes to the front of the choir and sings in the singular at certain points. Here is a leader of the people of God whose loyalty never falters and who casts himself on the covenant love of his Father in heaven, because he knows that his sufferings are not deserved—that it is for the sake of the reputation of God his Father that he must suffer these things. What a leader!

But, second, what about the plurals: "we", "our", and "us"? When we sing Psalm 44:9-12, it reminds us not to be surprised when we taste defeat as Jesus our leader did. Verses 13-16 help us feel the misery of shame: what it is to be mocked and laughed at. We need to understand shame as seen through biblical spectacles, so that when we take up the cross and experience something of this as followers of Jesus, we understand what is happening to us. And yet it is not our fault! So we take comfort, as we sing verses 17-22, that this is not a punishment for our sins. And, as the psalm closes, we pray and pray.

⌄ Apply

- ❓ *Have you ever experienced suffering or shame for the sake of God's honour?*
- ❓ *Do you know anyone experiencing this with whom you could share this psalm?*
- ❓ *How can you affirm your loyalty to the God of unfailing love this week?*

Bible in a year: Jeremiah 25-26 • Matthew 25 v 1-30 ✔

Glorious

How does God reveal his glory? In today's passage we read the stunning answer that through Christ, his glory is seen in you and me.

Seeing unveiled

Read 2 Corinthians 3:12-18

Moses put on a veil to prevent people seeing his face—and the glory of God, which is what had made it glow. His ministry could not reveal God's glory to people.

- ❓ *How does Paul compare this with reading the Old Testament without reference to Jesus (v 14-15)?*
- ❓ *What happens when you do turn to the Lord (v 16-17)?*
- ❓ *What is the result (v 18)?*
- ❓ *What does this mean for our ministry (v 12), and why?*

What Paul is saying here about our ministry is staggering. God reveals his glory to us in Christ through the gospel. When Christ is preached, God works by the Spirit to show people how gloriously beautiful Christ is. We should keep going because the ministry which God has given us reveals the glory of God in the face of Christ. There is no greater beauty, no greater privilege, no greater experience for human beings than this.

⌄ Apply

- ❓ *How could this make a difference to the way you approach...*
  - *reading the Bible?*
  - *teaching or supporting others?*
  - *praying?*
  - *your priorities for your life?*

Transformation

I wish I could change my physical appearance and character just by staring really hard at someone with more hair, a smaller nose, and more gifts and fewer faults. But it doesn't work like that—unless we are gazing at the Lord Jesus Christ in all his glory. According to Paul, as we gaze at Christ, we become like him.

- ❓ *What phrase does Paul use to describe what we are being transformed into (v 18)?*
- ❓ *In what aspects would you particularly like to be transformed to be like Christ?*

⌃ Pray

For yourself, your friends and family, and your church:

- Ask Jesus to show you how you can gaze at him more fully and consistently.

- Ask God to transform you by his Spirit, as he has promised to do.

- Pray that others might see God's glory through you, in what you say and do.

- Pray that because of the confidence you have in God's glory as revealed through Christ, you will be "very bold".

❤ *Bible in a year: Jeremiah 27-29 • Matthew 25 v 31-46*

Reasons to keep going

Chapter 4 is all about the secret of long-term, self-denying, Christ-honouring life ministry. Here we discover how to keep going and how not to lose heart.

Over the next two studies, we will see eight principles which will set us up to keep going in gospel ministry.

#1: It's a response to mercy
Read 2 Corinthians 4:1-2

By "ministry", Paul means everything we were looking at in 2:14 – 3:18: the life-giving, new-covenant, glory-revealing, character-transforming ministry of the Spirit through the gospel. God has given us a part in this ministry because he is immeasurably kind. Everything we do for him is good for us.

That's why we should do it with transparency and integrity ("setting forth the truth plainly", 4:2): because we are serving in the sight of the God who has shown us mercy.

#2: It's a battle
Read 2 Corinthians 4:3-4

❷ *What will get in the way of people understanding the message, even when we declare it openly and transparently?*

We are in a spiritual battle. Satan's influence is confined to "this world" or "this age"; but he still does his damnedest to keep people in the dark. Knowing that in advance will set us up better for the long haul.

#3: It's not about us
Read 2 Corinthians 4:5

❷ *What should we proclaim?*
❷ *What should be our attitude as we proclaim that?*
❷ *For whose sake are we proclaiming it?*

#4: It involves glory
Read 2 Corinthians 4:6

❷ *What two lights does Paul mention? Who do both come from?*
❷ *Why does knowing this about God and his work give us confidence in the knowledge we have of Christ?*

The more transfixed I am by Jesus in his death and resurrection, the more determined I am about gospel ministry. The more entranced I am with Jesus in his glory, the less likely I am to lose heart.

⌃ Pray

Reflecting on how you have seen God's kindness in your life, spend time thanking him.

Reflecting on how you have experienced the evil one's opposition to Christ, spend time asking for strength.

Reflecting on the cross, spend time praying for friends and family who don't yet know Christ.

Bible in a year: Jeremiah 30-31 • Matthew 26 v 1-25

More reasons

Do you ever think, "I'm just not strong enough for this"? Paul's remaining principles show us that our weakness was always planned for by God.

#5: We are weak

Read 2 Corinthians 4:7-12

- ❓ *What makes you feel like an unimpressive "jar of clay"?*
- ❓ *What does our weakness show (v 7)?*
- ❓ *How does Paul explain the way this works (v 8-9)?*

It isn't that God didn't realise that we would be so hopeless. He deliberately set things up in such a way that he works in our weakness.

The word "death" in verse 10 is an unusual one—referring to Jesus' whole journey through suffering up to and including the cross. Weakness and suffering are enduring characteristics of ministry. It's in our weakness that we can have life—and share it with others.

#6: Scripture helps

Read 2 Corinthians 4:13

Why speak? Because the Bible tells us to. Paul quotes Psalm 116:10. In this psalm, the psalmist is speaking honestly about the reality of his suffering; but he also speaks about God's goodness and salvation. The Bible reminds us that we can expect to suffer as we serve the Lord. Having realistic biblical expectations is a great help when it comes to keeping going!

#7: We will be raised

Read 2 Corinthians 4:14

- ❓ *What is Paul looking forward to?*
- ❓ *What has already happened to give Paul confidence in this?*

#8: The result is good

Read 2 Corinthians 4:15

- ❓ *What are the results of ministry in this verse?*
- ❓ *How does this help us not to lose heart, do you think?*

Therefore…

Read 2 Corinthians 4:16-18

- ❓ *Which other verses in chapter 4 is Paul summing up in each of these three verses?*

Grasping all these principles will completely reorient the way we look at the world (v 18). Throwing yourself into gospel ministry is hard, but every second of it will be worth it. We need not lose heart because we are spending our lives on the one thing that really matters.

⌄ Apply

- ❓ *Which friend(s) could you encourage with one or more of the truths from this passage?*

Looking to the future

What do the people you know look forward to? What do they hope for? The truth is that there is only one place to find real, lasting hope.

Groaning
Read 2 Corinthians 5:1-5

❓ *What are the two images Paul uses to describe our existence on earth?*

❓ *What do we "groan" about? Do you think we're right to do so?*

❓ *What are we looking forward to that is much better?*

The future will be great. Instead of fearing oblivion, we can look forward to the day when "what is mortal [is] swallowed up by life".

God himself has already guaranteed this—he has "paid the deposit" for the new creation by giving us the Holy Spirit. We experience the power and presence of God through the Spirit now, in a way that anticipates the full-blown version in the age to come.

⌄ Apply

❓ *How has the Spirit worked in your life, and what does that make you look forward to in the new creation?*

Good courage
Read 2 Corinthians 5:6-10

❓ *What's the disadvantage of being in our earthly bodies (v 6)?*

❓ *What makes this bearable (v 7)?*

To live by sight is to act as if we are in control and can fix things. It is to act as if position and reputation and appearance matter rather than clinging by faith to the fact that only the things of the Lord will last! To live by faith is to live to please Jesus, even now when we cannot see him.

When Paul says we will "receive what is due" (v 10), he doesn't mean that we should slip into a works-righteousness mindset, where we earn God's favour. No: we are already pleasing to God in Christ, and our reward will be given by grace. This is God's gentle encouragement to us to live to please him—imitating the One who has already defined what a life pleasing to God looks like, and who lived that life for us.

⌄ Apply

❓ *What "sights" do you cling to? How can you walk by faith instead?*

❓ *How can you make it your aim to please God while you are in this body?*

⌃ Pray

Pray for those you know who are clinging to hopes other than the one Paul describes.

Pray for those you know who are groaning because of the pains and frustrations of earthly life.

Recalibrating life

Who doesn't enjoy praise and recoil from criticism? Who would opt for a crushing rebuke rather than a pat on the back?

Who will we fear?
Read 2 Corinthians 5:11-15

Yet Paul says we are to fear God, not people.

Paul can live this way because his stance before God is one of simple, straightforward honesty. He is not pretending to be better than he actually is. He is saying, *Here I am, Lord—this is all I've got. I am what I am—and even then, it's only by your grace.*

> ❷ *Why is knowing that "what we are is plain to God" (v 11) both liberating and challenging?*
> ❷ *What does fearing God and not people's opinions look like for Paul (v 13)?*
> ❷ *What reasons does he give for having this attitude (v 14)?*

Living to please God frees up the apostle and his companions to love the Corinthians. They are not afraid to share the gospel, to take the initiative or to say the hard thing.

New creation

As Paul explains in verses 14-15, when we are united with Christ by faith in his death and resurrection, we have already died to ourselves. The only real option is to live for Christ.

Read 2 Corinthians 5:16-21

> ❷ *What impact should Christ's death and resurrection have on...*
> • *the way we treat other people (v 16)?*
> • *what we believe about Jesus (v 16)?*
> • *the way we view ourselves (v 17)?*

Verses 18-21 take us to the very heart of the gospel.

> ❷ *What has God done for us in Christ?*
> ❷ *What has he called us to do?*

Reconciliation means God has restored our relationship with him to one of delight and intimacy. That demanded a massive reversal: making "him who had no sin to be sin for us". Jesus Christ—God's perfect, flawless Son—became our sin-bearer, standing as our substitute and giving us his righteousness. It is a swap unlike any other because it actually brings about transformation.

Pray

This chapter calls us to recalibrate our lives.

> ❷ *Is any of these true of you?*
> • *You focus too much on the immediate, not on what's ahead.*
> • *You desire to please people more than God.*
> • *You struggle to love others selflessly.*
> • *You have given up on a relationship with a Christian brother or sister.*

Throw yourself on Christ for help. Then praise God! If you are in Christ, you are a new creation.

Make your mind up

In chapter 6, Paul's argument reaches its climax as he appeals to the Corinthians to stick with him and Christ.

Read 2 Corinthians 6:1-10

Act now

Here's a difficult reality: it's possible to receive the grace of God in vain. Paul's fear is that all his teaching of and investment in the Corinthians will come to nothing, and the gospel will have made no lasting difference in their lives.

The solution is in verse 2. Right now is the most acceptable time there is for embracing the gospel. That is also true today as we open the Bible. It falls on us right now to listen and respond.

Embrace reality

❷ Why does each of the things that Paul mentions in verses 4-10 serve to commend his ministry?

❷ Why does he think gospel ministry is worth it (v 8-10)?

❷ How would you sum up Paul's attitude to himself, to God, and to the Corinthians?

Paul desperately wants the Corinthians to get the fact that this is what authentic gospel ministry looks like. Paul goes to great lengths to make sure that no unnecessary difficulties are caused for other people (v 3)—that's why he puts up with so much.

If we have been mastered by the gospel, then it isn't about us any more but about other people. So we will do everything in our power to deal with anything about ourselves—what we say and how we live—that has any possibility of obscuring the gospel. Looking slick means nothing; it's about ensuring that the gospel is on full view and illustrated by every part of our lives.

⌄ Apply

❷ Is there anything you know God is addressing in your life that you have been avoiding thinking about? How could you act now for the gospel?

❷ Are you ready for the kind of hardship Paul describes in verses 4-5?

❷ Are you committed to the gospel-shaped means and methods Paul lists in verses 6-7?

❷ How do you cope with being honoured and dishonoured, being slandered and being praised (v 8)?

❷ Are you convinced that you can only find security and satisfaction in Christ, like Paul in verses 8-10?

⌃ Pray

Pray through this passage verse by verse. Think about where there are specific challenges for you. Ask for God's help in living his way and putting him first. Thank him for the promise of life and joy.

The king in the cave

Both Psalm 57 and Psalm 59 (which we'll look at on Day 89) are explicitly connected, as seen in their headings, with events in the early part of King David's life.

❷ *What do we learn about the setting of Psalm 57 from its heading?*

Read 1 Samuel 22:1-2 to discover the likely context that David was writing in.

King, but a refugee

The *heavenly reality* of his kingship was signified to King David by the anointing oil in 1 Samuel 16—he was God's chosen king. But his *earthly experience* as he wrote this psalm was one of being hated and hunted, a refugee in a cave. Did he wonder if it was all true?

❯ Apply

You know that God is in heaven and supreme; that God is love; that nothing in this life can threaten your eternal safety; that the Holy Spirit dwells within you. But do you ever wonder if the things of God are true?

❷ *How do you respond when your circumstances—family, work, health— don't seem to match the spiritual reality?*

Prayer from the cave

Read Psalm 57:1-11

❷ *What does David say about who God is and what he is like?*
❷ *What is David confident about (v 3)?*
❷ *What does he pray (v 5, 11)?*

Feel, trust, pray

In verse 6, David compares the pressures he feels to a hunter's trap: a pit and a net. He is deeply distressed—but somehow he is confident that by the end of the story, his enemies will "have fallen into it themselves". This confidence spills over into an exultant believing response to God's promises. David's heart is "steadfast" (v 7), and his mouth sings joyfully (v 7-8). So he prays again for the invisible God to make his presence felt all over the earth. Ultimately that can only happen when the anointed king sings the praises of God "among the nations" (v 9).

Words too big

David's words are too big for David's life. He sings of a day when the anointed King will sing God's praises all over the world. He sings by the Spirit of the Christ who was to come: the King on earth, upon whom the covenant love and faithfulness of God would rest in all its fullness, and in whom all the promises of the covenant would be "Yes!"

This King would know on earth the "cave" experience; indeed, finally the "cave tomb" experience, if that is not pressing the imagery too far. He would be the true anointed King, the Son of God, and yet he would be unrecognised, hated and hunted.

Meditate on how these words apply to King Jesus, and then turn those thoughts into prayers.

Being a temple

Should the Corinthians listen to Paul or to other teachers? It comes down to a simple contrast: who is for Christ and who is against him?

Read 2 Corinthians 6:11 – 7:1

Do not be yoked

- ❓ *What do we learn about Paul's approach to relationships with other Christians— including those where there is tension— in 6:11-13?*
- ❓ *But who does Paul tell the Corinthians to steer clear of in verses 14-18?*

Paul isn't offering a general template for relating to people who aren't Christians. This isn't about business partnerships or friendships. He is saying that those who oppose the truth of Christ are actually on the side of Satan (or "Belial", v 15): so how could we invite such teaching into Christ's church? The Corinthians must reject the pseudo-Christian teachers seeking to lead them astray.

☑ Apply

- ❓ *How much do you "open your heart" with other Christians—that is, be honest with them and committed to their good? Why? Does anything need to change?*
- ❓ *What alternative views of the world— involving lawless or dark or idolatrous or defiling attitudes or behaviour—do you need to steer clear of?*
- ❓ *How can you make sure you remain "separate" from the people who encourage such things and oppose the*

gospel (v 17), while not putting any obstacles to salvation in their way (v 3)?
- ❓ *Who do you need to pray for in the light of these verses?*

···· **TIME OUT** ·······································

Paul backs up these conclusions with a string of Old Testament quotations—Leviticus 26:11-12; Ezekiel 37:27; Isaiah 52:11; Ezekiel 20:41; and 2 Samuel 7:14—all drawn from contexts dealing with God's intimate relationship with his people, which was expressed and embodied by his presence in the temple.

Now that Christ has come, we are the temple—the place where God himself is and where he can be known and enjoyed— through our union with Christ.

This is all the more reason to be obedient. How could we trade in God's very presence for the sake of some second-rate philosophy that denies Christ?

Commit!

- ❓ *What is Paul's application of all this in 2 Corinthians 7:1?*
- ❓ *Why are we to seek holiness?*

This is not a game. God himself is speaking to us in the light of all that he has done and is doing and will do for us in the Lord Jesus. Let's commit ourselves to him afresh in repentance and faith.

Overflowing with joy

What does it take to be a happy servant of the Lord Jesus—even in the midst of suffering?

Read 2 Corinthians 7:2-4

Integrity

❓ *How has Paul acted towards the Corinthians (v 2)?*

It seems that Paul regularly examines himself to check on his tone, his content and his motives. We need to ask ourselves the same questions: Am I being too harsh (wronging people)? Am I being misleading in what I say (corrupting people)? Have I slipped into wanting more (taking advantage of people)?

Paul's integrity is the first step to being a happy gospel-worker. It frees him up to take the next step: investing in people.

Love

❓ *How does Paul think of the Corinthians (v 3-4)?*
❓ *What's the result of how Paul feels (v 4)?*

⏷ Apply

❓ *How does this compare with the way you view your fellow Christians?*
❓ *How could you be more like Paul, both in thought and deed?*

Joy

Read 2 Corinthians 7:5-9

❓ *Why was Paul afflicted (v 5)?*
❓ *What made him rejoice (v 6-7)?*

❓ *What made the Corinthians grieve (v 8)?*
❓ *Why has that made Paul rejoice (v 9)?*

Paul is committed to serving Christ with integrity, and he is determined to invest in people. So he is also willing to say what needs to be said—even if it is deeply unpopular. This is loving honesty. He didn't want to hurt the Corinthians, but he knew it was better for them if he spoke the truth.

John Chrysostom, a 4th-century bishop, wrote, "Like a father who watches his son being operated on, Paul rejoices not for the pain being inflicted, but for the cure which is the ultimate result".

The Corinthians felt the sting of Paul's words, they repented, and they changed—and that brought him joy!

⏶ Pray

How have you seen God work in the lives of your friends and family? If you are someone who struggles to feel happy, consider how you could keep reminding yourself of this as a way of finding comfort and joy.

Praise God for all he has done, and for the way he uses painful relationships and words as well as easy ones.

Pray for yourself: that you would be a comfort to other Christians by the way you love them, love God's truth, and repent of sin.

Godly grief

You wouldn't think grief could be the path to joy. But one particular type of grief always is.

....

Read 2 Corinthians 7:10-12

When life falls apart or people come face to face with sin, they have a variety of options. They might start making promises to a God who, up until five seconds before, they refused to believe in. They might try to deal with their feelings of guilt by going to church at Christmas or giving some money to charity. They might put on a performance of despair to elicit sympathy. But these are all forms of "worldly grief", and they lead to death.

❓ *What kind of grief is God looking for instead (v 10)?*
❓ *What does this lead to (v 11)?*

When real repentance happens, we know. The tears are real, the words are humble, the determination is obvious, the change is authentic. And the joy is real.

This is the type of grief that Paul was hoping to provoke by his letter (v 12).

⌃ Pray

Use the Ten Commandments in **Exodus 20:1-17**, Jesus' commands in **Matthew 22:34-40**, and Paul's instructions in **Galatians 5:16-26** to help you consider what you may need to repent of. Pray that your godly grief may lead to all that Paul describes in 2 Corinthians 7:10-11.

Perfect confidence

Read 2 Corinthians 7:13-16

Paul had been waiting for Titus to show up (2:13) and was comforted by his coming (7:6)—and not only by his coming but by the news he brought.

❓ *What had Paul said to Titus previously (v 14)?*
❓ *What did Titus find when he met the Corinthians, and what impact did that have on him?*
❓ *What did Paul think when he heard about this from Titus?*

⌄ Apply

Paul rejoices not only because the Corinthians have lived up to his boasting about them, but also because, when they have failed to live up to it, they showed genuine grief and repentance. The obedience Titus has seen (v 15) is all the more wonderful because it was not always the case.

❓ *Does it surprise you that this is what Paul rejoices at?*
❓ *Why is repentance such a joyful thing for him?*
❓ *When you feel downcast, like Paul in verse 5, what comforts you?*
❓ *How could you help yourself to rejoice more in your own repentance, and in the repentance of others?*

Gospel generosity

In chapter 8 Paul begins the longest, most rigorous, most sustained treatment of a gospel-shaped attitude to money in the whole Bible.

Why? Because he needed money. It's easy to forget that these are real letters, written to real people for pressing and urgent reasons. Paul wanted the Corinthians to give so that their poor brothers and sisters could eat.

But that isn't Paul's only motive.

Read 2 Corinthians 8:1-7

> ❷ *What does Paul want the Corinthians to know about (v 1)?*
> ❷ *What is the evidence of this (v 2)?*

The churches of Macedonia have blown Paul away with their selfless generosity, and he knows this can only come from the grace of God.

> ❷ *How do we see that this giving is sacrificial?*
> ❷ *How do we see that this giving is spiritual and God-oriented?*

Giving to God

The idea of joyful giving is a strange concept for most of us. But the Macedonians actually begged to be allowed to give! That's because they knew that giving money to other believers was the overflow of giving themselves to the Lord.

Ultimately, this passage isn't about money— it's about living for Jesus.

That's why Paul tells the Corinthians to give like the Macedonians, and he has sent Titus to see through the possibility of a collection among them (v 6). They have an opportunity to put their money where their mouth is.

Gain and loss

We usually think something is lost when we give it away. The Macedonians had been freed up by the gospel, and so they realised that to give, even in their poverty, is to gain, not to lose.

☑ Apply

> ❷ *How do you think you would have felt to have received this letter from Paul?*
> ❷ *How easy do you find it to give away money or possessions?*
> ❷ *Does it help to think of giving money as a way of giving yourself to God?*
> ❷ *What do you think would happen if you gave as generously as the Macedonians?*

⌃ Pray

Pray for the ministries which you or your church support financially. Thank God for the grace to give. Pray that he would show you whether your own giving needs to change in any way.

Giving like Jesus

Things are rarely black and white when it comes to money. So Paul's tone in today's passage is persuasive rather than commanding.

But his concern is that the Corinthians would display real selflessness, which would lead to the strengthening of others.

Read 2 Corinthians 8:8-15

Paul starts by reminding the Corinthians of the comparison he has just made with the Macedonians and their "earnestness".

Then he pulls out his biggest theological gun and tells them to act like Jesus (v 9).

❓ *How many ways can you think of in which Jesus "became poor" for our sake?*

Follow through

In particular, the Corinthians need to follow through on their pledges (v 10-11). If you say you are going to support someone financially, then go and fill out the forms. If you say you're going to pray for someone, do it straight away. If you say you are going to show up somewhere, then make sure you are there. Follow through on your commitments. Why? Because Jesus did.

❓ *What can get in the way of doing what we have committed to do?*

❓ *Who do we tend to be prioritising in those situations?*

❓ *How is that different to Christ's attitude?*

Fairness

❓ *How does Paul say that things will be made fair (v 12-14)?*

Paul's ideal is that Christian believers would choose to put others first, caring for each other when they can—in a kind of grace-driven equilibrium. Nobody is keeping score, but there is a natural ebb and flow as we live together in dependence, without either shame, which would stop us asking for help, or greed, which would stop us giving it.

In verse 15, Paul supports this principle with Exodus 16:18, which is about the manna in the wilderness. God gave just the right amount: no more, no less.

We usually spend as much as we can afford on ourselves. But Paul says that the way of Christ is to lavish whatever we can on others for the sake of the gospel.

⌃ Pray

Thank God for the ways in which he has provided for you.

Ask him to help you to see where you could be generous with what you have.

If you are in need, ask him to provide what you lack through your brothers and sisters.

An earnest appeal

Asking for money often feels awkward—and it did for Paul as much as it does for us.

It's hard enough to sort out one motive from another within ourselves, let alone persuade others that we really are honest and worth giving money to.

In today's passage, Paul describes three men whom the Corinthians can really trust.

Read 2 Corinthians 8:16-24

Servant hearts

❷ *What does Paul admire about Titus (v 16-17)?*

❷ *What does he admire about the brother who he talks about in verse 18?*

❷ *What does he say about the other brother who he mentions in verse 22?*

This party of three was appointed by "the churches" (v 19)—presumably the key churches in Macedonia—to collect money and make sure that the gift was received, so that the church in Jerusalem would be encouraged and God himself glorified.

Paul doesn't tell us the names of these two other brothers names because that isn't the point. The point is that, along with Titus, these two men are committed to serving in and through the gospel.

Beyond reproach

❷ *What two reasons does Paul give for collecting the money in person (v 19)?*

❷ *What wrong impression does he worry that people will have (v 20)?*

❷ *But what does he insist is his aim (v 21)?*

For Paul, it is an absolute non-negotiable that things are done properly—that is, in a way which brings honour to God and also doesn't drag the church needlessly into disrepute. He knows that fights and accusations about money will kill off gospel ministry more quickly than almost anything else. When it comes to money, we need to be beyond reproach, because only then will people be able to see that the gospel produces genuine servant-heartedness.

This is not so that we are recognised as honourable for our own sake but so that nothing hinders the gospel.

❷ *In each of the descriptions of the three men, how do we see true gospel-centred servant-heartedness?*

☑ Apply

❷ *How do people who make appeals for money nowadays compare with Paul and the brothers he describes? Does that affect your decision about whether or not to give?*

❷ *What mixed motives do you have when you spend or give money? How could you make sure you are beyond reproach?*

O God, my fortress

As with Psalm 57 (Day 82), this psalm is set in the time when David was God's anointed king but was being hunted by King Saul.

Read 1 Samuel 18:20-21, 28-29; 19:11-17

❓ *Why did Saul agree to his daughter Michal marrying David (18:21)?*

❓ *Who saved David from Saul (19:11-17)?*

❓ *Who was really keeping David safe (18:28)?*

Read Psalm 59

❓ *What repetitions do we find in this psalm (v 6 and 14, v 9-10 and 17)?*

Verses 1-10 are punctuated by threat (v 6-7) but conclude with confidence (v 9-10). Verses 11-17 are substantially parallel to verses 1-10. As we go through these verses, I think the psalm will teach us two things:

• We will learn to shiver at the lurking threat of evil. This will help us feel more deeply the harder part of walking in the footsteps of Jesus our King.

• We will be taught to pray confidently for the visible victory of God's King. Following Jesus is a paradoxical experience: it is hard now, but it will end with his victory and ours!

❓ *How does David's prayer in verses 1-4 crescendo in intensity?*

David is surrounded. There is no way out. The new truth that David introduces in verses 3-4 is his own innocence. Like the Lord Jesus after him, he is guilty of "no offence or sin ... no wrong". David can plead, "Arise" (v 4) because he is in covenant with God and he is righteous. He is not asking God to

do something arbitrary; he calls upon God to uphold justice.

❓ *What is David confident about (v 9-10)?*

❓ *What needs to be known "to the end of the earth" (v 13)?*

The second cycle begins with a surprising prayer (v 11-13). Somehow the defeat of the king's enemies needs to be clear, public and unambiguous. The conclusion that onlookers must draw is "that God rules"— that Psalm 2 is true. And this must become known "to the ends of the earth".

The New Testament teaches us that the final public victory was achieved at the cross of Jesus Christ. It was there that Jesus "disarmed the powers and authorities [and] made a public spectacle of them, triumphing over them by the cross" (Colossians 2:15). When the perfect King was surrounded, hounded, done to death and then raised bodily from the dead, the whole universe could know that sin and death have lost their sting and all the powers of evil have been defeated.

☑ Apply

❓ *While being honest about days of darkness, how can you also make sure that you are clear about the confidence you have in Christ?*

❓ *Do you think you are as passionate as the psalmist about the rule of God's King? How do you need to pray for God to help you change?*

Gospel integrity

You know what you need to do, says Paul—now get on and do it.

Others have been encouraged by the Corinthians' loud pledges—but now the time has come to deliver. The Corinthians either have to come up with the money or there will be humiliation all round.

Be ready
Read 2 Corinthians 9:1-4

- ❓ *Why does Paul not bother describing the ministry which the money will pay for (v 1-2)?*
- ❓ *What impact has Paul's confidence in the Corinthians had (v 2)?*
- ❓ *But what is his worry (v 4)?*

For Paul, the failure of the Corinthians to come through on their word would be a very big deal indeed. He puts his reputation and relationship on the line—if they fail to keep their promise, then they will be shaming Paul, who had trusted their word and made promises to others on their behalf.

Underneath this is the principle that the gospel produces integrity. God has spoken to us reliably and kept every promise he makes, so we need to make every effort to speak reliably to others.

- ❓ *Do you think Paul was right to boast about the Corinthians' generosity?*
- ❓ *What would you have felt if you had been among the Corinthians reading this letter?*

Be cheerful
Read 2 Corinthians 9:5-7

The phrase "not as ... grudgingly given" (v 5) could be translated as "not as an expression of stinginess". The gift is to be free, generous, and ready when Titus gets there. They are to make up their minds about how much they will give, and then give it willingly.

- ❓ *What two reasons does Paul give for this in verses 6-7?*

We tend to live by a different and more worldly proverb: God gives credit to a reluctant but careful giver. In verse 7, Paul seems to have something a little freer, a little more lavish, in mind. When it comes to giving, extravagance is good!

So, when we can't give, let's make sure we see it as Paul does—as missing out.

⌄ Apply

- ❓ *What difference has it made to you when people have followed through on their word?*
- ❓ *In what areas of your life could you be a better model of that kind of integrity?*
- ❓ *What stops you from making up your mind about how much to give, and then giving it cheerfully?*

Ask for God's help in making you into a cheerful giver.

Abundance

What do you fear missing out on? And what would make missing out worthwhile?

The kind of gospel-shaped life that leads us to give generously will not feel like missing out. Why? Because God will continue to supply us with whatever we need to get on with the work of the gospel.

Read 2 Corinthians 9:8-15

❷ What does Paul think is the best of God's gifts?

❷ How does he show this in verses 8 and 10?

Our God loves to drench us with good things. But he does not give any blanket guarantees of either wealth or health. Paul's allusions in verse 10—to Isaiah 55:10, which is primarily about God's word, and to Hosea 10:12, which is about righteousness—show that he has moved far beyond finance to the way in which God works in and through the gospel. If God enriches us, it is to make us generous (2 Corinthians 9:11).

This is why we can afford to give generously. It isn't that we give and God gives back to us, or that he gives more, or anything like that. Our giving demonstrates that we believe the gospel and trust God to do us good, in riches or poverty.

⌄ Apply

❷ Who should we thank when we have enough to eat?

❷ What about when we see ourselves being kind, good and generous?

The net result

❷ What are the effects of the gifts of generosity and good works (v 11-14)...
   • on the Corinthians?
   • on those receiving their gifts?
   • on God?

❷ Which of these things do you think is most surprising or counter-cultural?

❷ Which do you find most compelling and motivating?

The solid commitment that the Corinthians have shown by giving their money will spill over into prayer, as God's people cry together, "Thanks be to God for his indescribable gift!" (v 15).

❷ What gifts could Paul include in his prayer of thanksgiving? Think about both spiritual gifts and material gifts, given both to individuals and to groups of people.

❷ How many of these gifts could we thank God for today?

⌃ Pray

Thank God for his indescribable gift to us in the gospel of the Lord Jesus Christ, and for all the abundance which that includes.

Ask God for his help in living in the light of this deep generosity.

THE VICTORY OF THE CROSS
IN FOUR WORDS

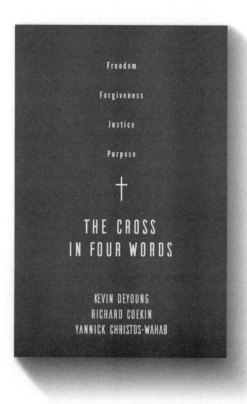

This foundational book by Kevin DeYoung, Richard
Coekin and Yannick Christos-Wahab looks at shadows
of the cross in the Old Testament to sum up the victory
of the cross in four words. Enjoy the glory of the
achievement of the cross—and see what that means
for you personally.

thegoodbook.co.uk/fourwords
thegoodbook.com/fourwords

STRENGTH FOR YOUR MARRIAGE
IN TIMES OF TRIAL

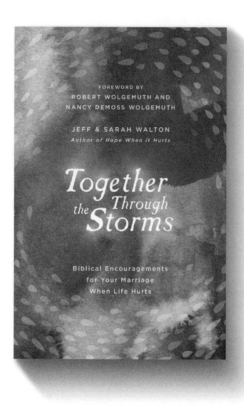

This devotional book helps married couples to navigate the storms of life together. Sarah Walton (co-author of *Hope when it Hurts*) and her husband, Jeff, share their own experiences and, as they work through the book of Job, encourage couples to lift their eyes above their trials, off their spouse, and onto our all-sufficient Saviour.

**thegoodbook.co.uk/storms
thegoodbook.com/storms**

Introduce a friend to

explore

If you're enjoying using *Explore*, why not introduce a friend? *Time with God* is our introduction to daily Bible reading and is a great way to get started with a regular time with God. It includes 28 daily readings along with articles, advice and practical tips on how to apply what the passage teaches.

Why not order a copy for someone you would like to encourage?

Coming up next...

❤ Philippians
with Tim Thornborough

❤ Joshua
with Jon Gemmell

❤ Daniel
with Carl Laferton & Rachel Jones

❤ 2 Corinthians 10 – 13
with Gary Millar & Katy Morgan

❤ Jude
with Carl Laferton

❤ Psalms
with Christopher Ash & Alison Mitchell